Solving
Sherlock Holmes

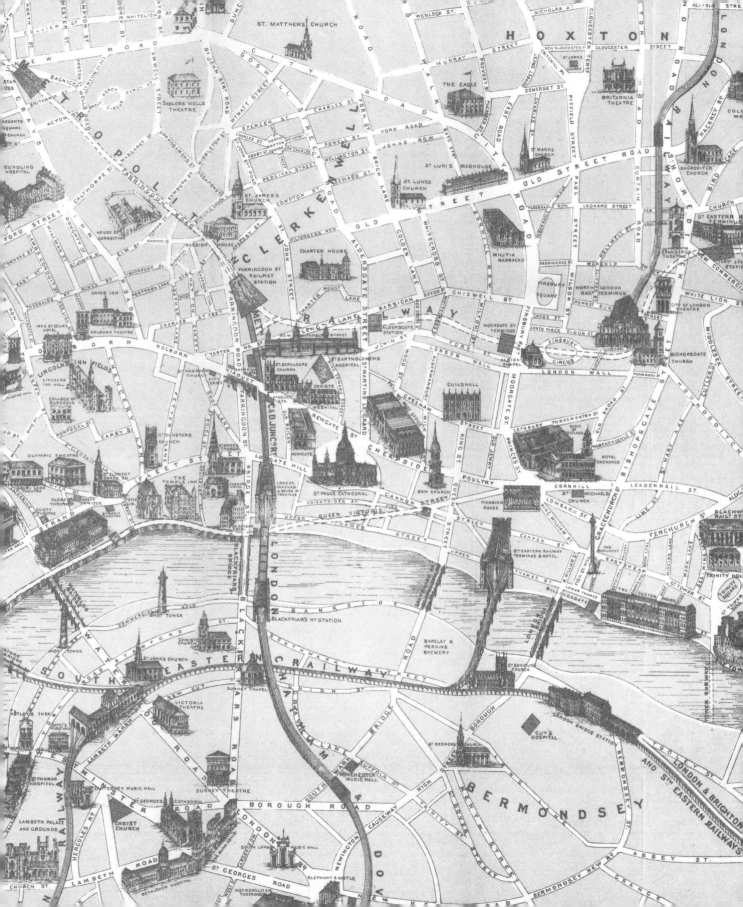

Solving
Sherlock Holmes

Puzzle Your Way Through the Cases

Pierre Berloquin

WELLFLEET
PRESS

Inspiring | Educating | Creating | Entertaining

Brimming with creative inspiration, how-to projects, and useful information to enrich your everyday life, Quarto Knows is a favorite destination for those pursuing their interests and passions. Visit our site and dig deeper with our books into your area of interest: Quarto Creates, Quarto Cooks, Quarto Homes, Quarto Lives, Quarto Drives, Quarto Explores, Quarto Gifts, or Quarto Kids.

First published in 2017 by Wellfleet Press, an imprint of The Quarto Group, 142 West 36th Street, 4th Floor, New York, NY 10018, USA
T (212) 779-4972 **F** (212) 779-6058 **www.QuartoKnows.com**

Wellfleet Press titles are also available at discount for retail, wholesale, promotional, and bulk purchase. For details, contact the Special Sales Manager by email at specialsales@quarto.com or by mail at The Quarto Group, Attn: Special Sales Manager, 401 Second Avenue North, Suite 310, Minneapolis, MN 55401, USA.

Layout: Didier Guiserix
Art: Denis Dugat and Didier Guiserix (based on Sidney Paget's original works)
London Map: Nicku/Shutterstock.com
Game Concept and Book Design: Pierre Berloquin – Créalude

For their invaluable help, the author would like to thank Louise Wallace, Mike Dickman, and Stuart Miller.

10 9 8 7 6 5 4 3 2 1

ISBN: 978-1-57715-146-3

Printed in China

Contents

Introduction

Do not read this book. Play it!

Instead of reading each chapter chronologically, page after page—like a traditional book—and solving each puzzle as you go, skip around, instead, and have more fun following Holmes's trail using the clues, events, and puzzles hidden in the following pages, like our famous detective would do when solving a case! There are three intertwined challenges awaiting you.

Challenge 1: Every chapter contains twenty-three puzzles that Holmes and Watson must solve. They react to famous characters, surroundings, and unusual events that were inspired by six classic Sherlock Holmes stories. For extra enjoyment, the plots have been slightly reimagined to add further mystery and purposely create more hurdles than Holmes and Watson had to overcome in the original stories.

Challenge 2: Each chapter contains a map. Tear it out and keep it next to you as you work through the puzzles. After you solve a puzzle, part of the answer, or sometimes a hint, is enclosed within a box at the bottom of the page. The answer will lead you to the next puzzle that you must solve. You will move around the map, like through a maze, and skip around the puzzles.

Challenge 3: Hidden in each chapter is one intentional letter mistake to keep you on your toes. At first glance it may appear to be typo, or perhaps a misspelling, but it is not! Each letter (a total of six) will spell out a final word when all the puzzles have been completed.

Best of luck!

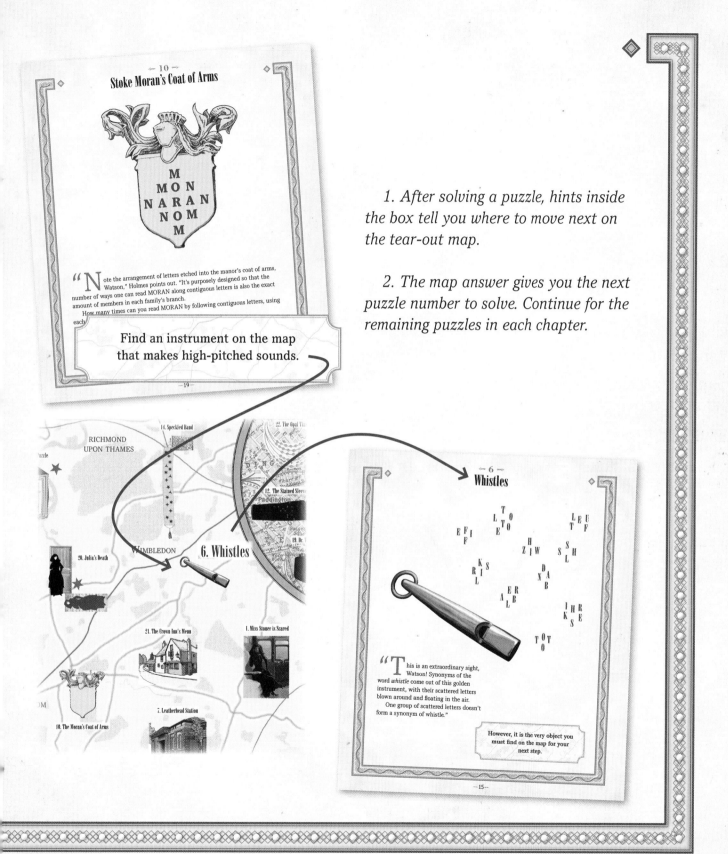

— 10 —
Stoke Moran's Coat of Arms

M
O N
M O N
N A R A N
O M
N O M

"Note the arrangement of letters etched into the manor's coat of arms, Watson," Holmes points out. "It's purposely designed so that the number of ways one can read MORAN along contiguous letters is also the exact amount of members in each family's branch.

How many times can you read MORAN by following contiguous letters, using each

Find an instrument on the map
that makes high-pitched sounds.

— 19 —

1. After solving a puzzle, hints inside the box tell you where to move next on the tear-out map.

2. The map answer gives you the next puzzle number to solve. Continue for the remaining puzzles in each chapter.

RICHMOND
UPON THAMES

14. Speckled Band

22. The Opal T

Puzzle

12. The Stained Sleev
Paddington

20. Julia's Death

WIMBLEDON

6. Whistles

19. Dr.

21. The Crown Inn's Menu

1. Miss Stoner is Scared

OM

7. Leatherhead Station

10. The Moran's Coat of Arms

— 6 —
Whistles

"This is an extraordinary sight, Watson! Synonyms of the word *whistle* come out of this golden instrument, with their scattered letters blown around and floating in the air.

One group of scattered letters doesn't form a synonym of whistle."

However, it is the very object you
must find on the map for your
next step.

— 15 —

CHAPTER 1

The Adventure of the Speckled Band

Sir Arthur Conan Doyle, author and creator of our famous detective, chose this short story as his favorite Sherlock Holmes adventure. Blending intrigue, action, and logic into one, it is a perfect mystery recipe that readers have loved since it was published in 1883. In fact, Conan Doyle liked it so much that he dramatized it into a play, which was met with as much success as the original story. Here, "The Adventure of the Speckled Band" is our first voyage to Holmes's imaginary land. It takes place in London's Baker Street, in addition to the story's manor estate of Stoke Moran, near Leatherhead in Surrey. The characters travel back and forth by train and horse carts as the story develops.

As explained in the introduction, tear out the map attached to this chapter and keep it with you as a travel guide. It will be essential for steering you through the strange places and events within this chapter.

Start with the first puzzle on the next page, solve it, and then follow the boxed hint to find the next puzzle number on the map. With the puzzle's number above the title, go to the corresponding puzzle in the chapter.

Repeat this sequence with each puzzle, going back and forth from the puzzles to the map and back again, until you reach the last case.

1

Miss Stoner Is Scared

Early one April morning, a young woman sits on a train headed to London dressed in black and heavily veiled. Feeling agitated and frightened, Miss Stoner is on her way to meet and seek the help and advice from the famous detective Sherlock Holmes. She holds a glass cube—a gift from her late twin sister—which contains one letter of Miss Stoner's common first name etched onto 5 sides. Upon her arrival, Holmes immediately wakes up his friend and associate Dr. John Watson.

"Very sorry to wake you up abruptly, Watson," Holmes says while standing next to his bed, "but a young lady has arrived in a considerable state of excitement, and insists upon seeing me.

"She is holding a peculiar cube with letters. Can you decipher the name on it?"

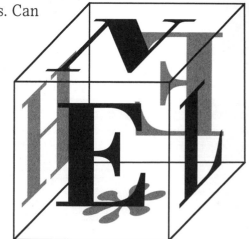

Look for Waterloo Station
on the map.

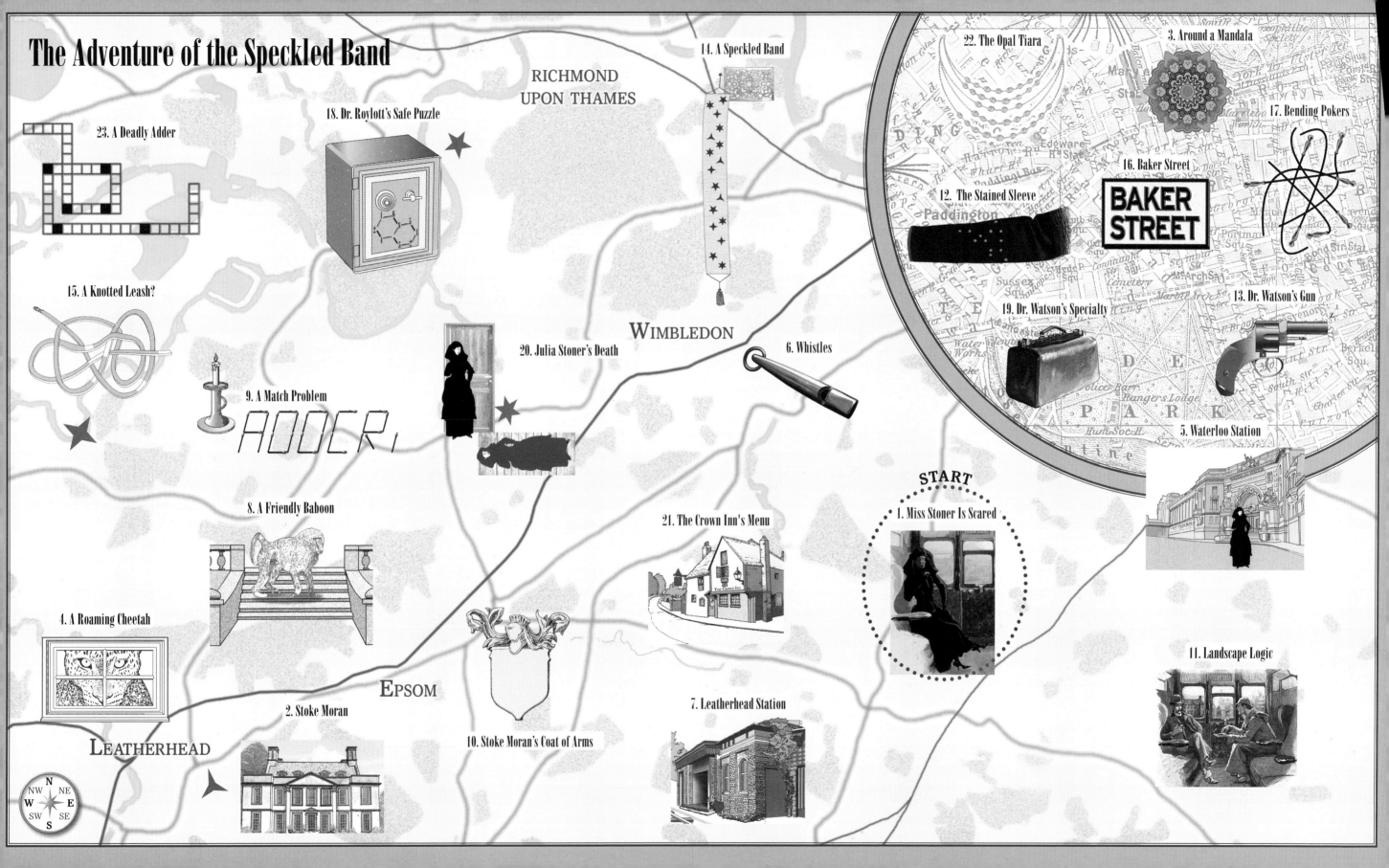

MAP

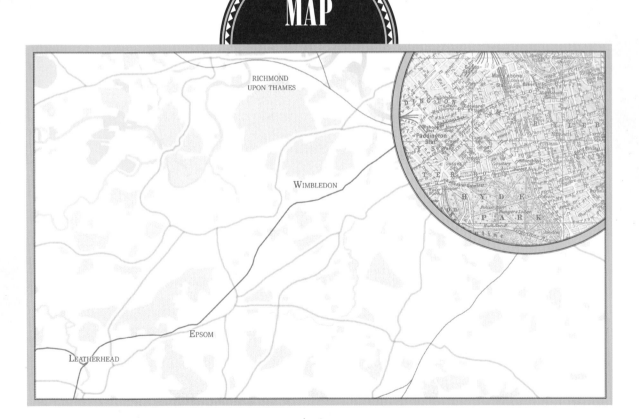

BAKER
STREET

U pon arriving at Stoke Moran, the mansion and estate of Helen Stoner's stepfather, Dr. Roylott, our famous detective's trained eye instantly imagines a puzzle.

He asks Watson, "What if some of the sections of the manor were moved around in a circle, with each piece replacing the one following it? Would you be able to rearrange them correctly?"

The number of displaced parts tells you where to go on the map.

Around a Mandala

21   13

7   14

35   28

U pon hearing that Dr. Roylott had been a medical practitioner in Calcutta, India, Sherlock proposes a game for Watson.

"Mandalas are popular symbolic pictures in Calcutta. Despite the logic within the numbers, what is the odd number out?"

Go to the odd number
out on the map

A Roaming Cheetah

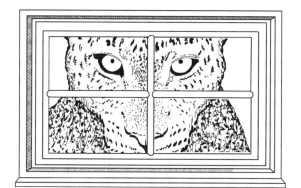

TIGER
TION
JAGUAR
LEOPARD
CARACAL
SERVAL
COLOCOLO
KODKOD
OCELOT
ONCILLA
LYNX
BOBCAT
MARGAY
COUGAR
CAT
CHEETAH

"Do not feel threatened, Watson," Sherlock exclaims. "That cheetah is looking at us through the window out of sheer curiosity, I'm sure. It is certainly tame and means us no harm. I would not say the same of all felines, though."

This remark sets Holmes and Watson off, putting together their knowledge of felines and making a list of the species they can recall. All but one in the list to the right can be found in the word search below, from right to left, left to right, or vertically.

D	N	R	E	G	I	T	H	C	T	A	C
N	O	I	L	E	U	R	C	G	U	O	C
R	A	U	Y	A	L	E	O	P	A	R	D
D	E	Z	N	O	Z	R	U	R	A	M	F
P	I	D	X	O	J	A	G	U	A	R	S
C	A	R	A	C	A	L	A	E	A	L	E
A	T	O	L	E	C	O	R	R	E	O	R
C	O	L	O	C	O	L	O	I	H	C	V
C	U	N	N	A	K	O	D	K	O	D	A
C	H	E	E	T	A	H	T	T	O	R	L
T	A	C	B	O	B	M	A	R	G	A	Y

The rank of the missing feline from above will tell you where to go on the map.

H elen Stoner hurries out of London Waterloo Station, looking for a cab. Her mind is so deeply troubled that she becomes disoriented within her surroundings. Holmes sketches the picture above to depict some sections of the train station that her mind flipped horizontally under the stress and challenges Watson.

"Can you count the sections that did not move or flip?"

Find Sherlock Holmes's street in London on the map and go there.

"This is an extraordinary sight, Watson! Synonyms of the word *whistle* come out of this golden instrument, with their scattered letters blown around and floating in the air.

"Can you find one group of scattered letters that doesn't form a synonym of whistle?"

Find this object on the map
for your next step.

Leatherhead Station

6 : 32
8 : 25
9 : 33
10 : 25
12 : 26
12 : 43
15 : 53
18 : 36
20 : 54

"Look here, Watson. What do you make of this illogical timetable of trains to London Waterloo Station?
"One train simply doesn't belong. Which one is it?"

The line number of the illogical train in the timetable tells you where to go on the map.

A Friendly Baboon

BABOON
MACAQUE
COLOBUS
SAKI
DRILL
GEMLADA
UAKARI
MARMOSET
LESULA
MANDRILL
PATAS
ROLOWAY
TAMARIN
TITI
CAPUCHIN
VERVET

"There's a baboon," said Holmes. "Hardly an exception among monkeys except for its unusually long nose.

"I owned a monkey once. It happens to be the twelfth one in the list if you can imagine it set in alphabetical order."

Holmes's monkey's rank
in the above list tells you
where to go on the map.

A Match Problem

Sherlock explains to Watson, "While dying, Julia Stoner understood what was killing her. She tried to leave a clue for her sister using a box of matches next to a candle.

"She almost succeeded, but only one match is yet to be in its right place. Can you figure it out?"

Move one match to write the
name of what killed Julia,
then look for it on the map.

Stoke Moran's Coat of Arms

"Note the arrangement of letters etched into the manor's coat of arms, Watson," Holmes points out. "It's purposely designed so that the number of ways one can read MORAN along contiguous letters is also the exact amount of members in each family's branch.

"How many times can you read MORAN by following contiguous letters, using each letter only once per word?"

Find an instrument on the map
that makes high-pitched sounds.

Landscape Logic

While on the train to Leatherhead and admiring the passing mansions and landscape, Holmes challenges Watson to a logic game with the following facts:

(1) Mansions with walls covered with honeysuckle do not have tiled roofs.
(2) Whenever there is a pine tree, there is honeysuckle on the walls.
(3) Brick walls always go with tiled roofs.

He asks, "Given the above facts, can any of the mansions have a pine tree in front of a brick wall?"

Find their destination
on the map.

The Stained Sleeve

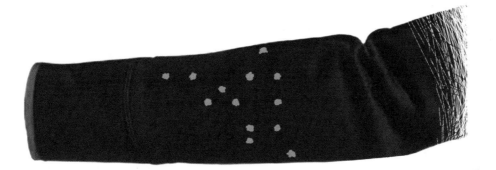

Looking at the mud stains on Helen Stoner's sleeve, Holmes brilliantly deduces that she was driven to the train station in a dog cart. However, he remains silent for a few minutes and stares at the stains. He then asks Watson, "I can't help but wonder how many straight lines could be drawn through the centers of at least three stains.

"Similar to the one displayed, how many lines can you draw, Watson?"

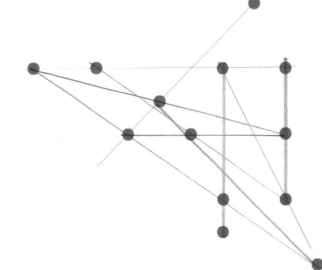

Find a magnificent
jewel on the map
and go there.

Dr. Watson's Gun

**THE MAIN PARTS
OF THIS GUN ARE:**

**BARREL
LATCH
CYLINDER
FRAME
HAMMER
SCREW
PIN
TRIGGER
GUARD
GRIP
AXIS**

"Some of the words in the list stand out because one or more of their letters is not in any other word," Sherlock explains to Watson. "For example, x in axis cannot be hound in any other word.

"Which other words fit in that category?"

Add 5 to the total number of
such words to know where
to go next on the map.

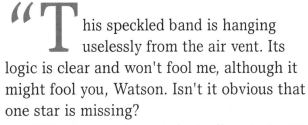

"This speckled band is hanging uselessly from the air vent. Its logic is clear and won't fool me, although it might fool you, Watson. Isn't it obvious that one star is missing?

"What type of star is logically missing?"

Find the missing star on the map. The place you should go next is near the star.

"Aha, a tangled leash, Watson,
the very depiction of your mind
when working out a puzzle!" Holmes jokes
with Watson. "I wrote a book about knots
a while back, since they many times help
identify a criminal's trade or hometown.

"This dog leash may, or may not, be
able to become a knot. What do you think,
Watson?"

Find the candle
Julia Stoner held
before she
died and go there
on the map.

Arriving back to Baker Street, Sherlock notices that several cracks in the wall have developed behind his Baker Street plaque.
He asks Watson, "How many triangles can be created from them if the plaque wasn't covering them?"

Find Dr. Watson's bag
on the map.

Bending Pokers

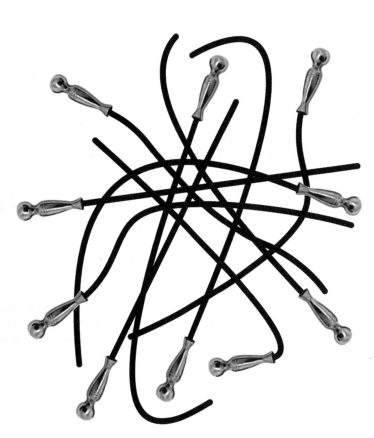

Dr. Roylott, Helen Stoner's stepfather, marches suddenly into Sherlock Holmes's office. Trying to intimidate the detective with his physical strength, Dr. Roylott bends a fire poker with his bare hands. But, instead of being impressed, Holmes makes fun of him.

Seizing a pencil and a sheet of paper, he quickly draws a set of shapes, saying, "If you had an ounce of creativity, doctor, you would have bent the poker in more clever shapes like these."

"But Sherlock," interrupts Watson, "not all of your shapes are unique; some are identical."

"Indeed, Watson, you are right. I did repeat myself a few times. How many identical pairs can you find?"

Go to the puzzle to the
immediate northwest of this
one on the map.

"Can you guess the lock combination, Watson?" Holmes asks. "That saucer of milk beside Dr. Roylott's safe is a bizarre sight. It leads us to think that the contraption serves a different, unusual purpose. If we were to suppose it doesn't store money or valuables, like regular safes, what, then, could it contain? Something that consumes milk, perhaps? But certainly not the cheetah!"

Holmes continues, "Interesting, it also appears Dr. Roylott has a playful sense of humor, for, as a reminder, he etched onto the safe's door a puzzle, whose solution must be the lock's combination—playful but unsafe, I must say!"

Find the logical combination number, add 11, and move there on the map.

Dr. Watson's Specialty

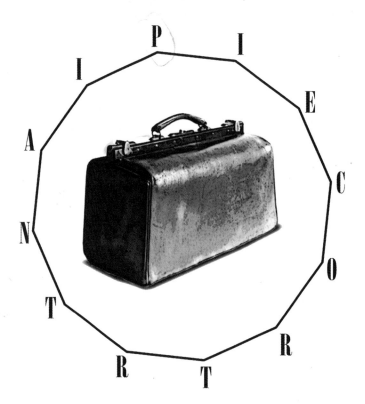

A t 221B Baker Street, Helen Stoner meets Dr. Watson.

To figure out his occupation on this polygon, Sherlock challenges her.

"Start on P and then keep skipping over the same number of letters to spell out Watson's specialty," he hints to her.

Find on the map a part of Helen Stoner's clothing where Sherlock Holmes sees a clue.

"Julia died a mysterious death in front of her twin sister, Helen. Looking at her sister, Helen noticed several differences in the outlines of her own dress and that of her sister's," Holmes explains.

"The twins are identical—except for their clothes. How many differences can you see?" he asks Watson.

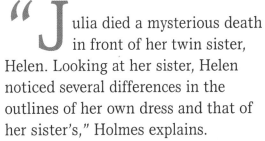

Go to the place on the map where Holmes and Watson have dinner.

The Crown Inn's Menu

In front of the Crown Inn, Holmes delightedly exclaims, "Are these people expecting me? Their menu obviously challenges me to a battle of wits.

"The price of the last dish is missing, but I can figure it out easily from the other prices, which are clearly logical.

"Can you work out the missing price, Watson?"

Menu

Pigeon Souffle	6/7
Fricando Veal	8/4
Pork Griskins	4/8
House Lambs	5/5
Devilled Fowl	8/4
French Pye	???? 6/3

Once determined, the number on the left side of the price plus 9 will tell you where to go to next on the map.

The Opal Tiara

"I remember that tiara clearly from the Farrington case" says Holmes, "for the jeweler added a touch of logic to its perfect beauty. There's a method in his selection of stones and the way he strung them onto golden chains.

"However, one chain is not arranged like the others. Which one is it, Watson?"

Find a set of bent fire pokers on the map and head there.

A Deadly Adder

ADDER

ANACONDA

ASP

COBRA

KEELBACK

MAMBA

URUTU

VIPER

YARARA

"One can easily imagine snake names written on this speckled-band crossword. When one thinks of all the snakes Dr. Roylott could have used, Watson, it seems like our planet is swarming with them."

Fill in the squares with the snakes listed above to conclude the adventure and then read the next page.

Chapter Clue

"Did you notice a tiny but strange mistake in this chapter, Watson? Ah, of course, you couldn't see it because your mind is not trained to notice the small discrepancies that I, as a detective, call clues. These details, generally unheeded by ordinary mortals, are the essential stones on which I build my solutions to the mysteries."

The anomaly you found in this chapter is a clue to the final word puzzle. Make a note of the letter and save it below to solve the puzzle on page 163, after you have gone through the six adventures in the book.

Clue for chapter 1: _____

CHAPTER 2

The Adventure
of the Dancing Men

The immense popularity of this adventure is only partly due to Conan Doyle's talent. Its renown, in fact, is largely due to its use of a secret code featuring symbols of dancing men to represent letters. It appeared sixty years after Edgar Allan Poe's *The Gold-Bug*, which was the first story built around decoding of a cipher. While Poe used typographic characters, Doyle's dancing silhouettes are much more pleasant to the eye and more intriguing.

As explained in the introduction, tear out the map attached to this chapter and keep it with you as a travel guide. It will be essential for steering you through the strange places and events within this chapter.

Start with the first puzzle on the next page, solve it, and then follow the boxed hint to find the next puzzle number on the map. With the puzzle's number above the title, go to the corresponding puzzle in the chapter.

Repeat this sequence with each puzzle, going back and forth from the puzzles to the map and back again, until you reach the last case.

An Experiment

"Look closely, Watson," Holmes instructs. "While waiting for our next client, a Mr. Hilton Cubitt from Norfolk County, I'm using the free time to conduct an experiment. In many criminal cases, chemistry can be essential for exposing the truth. I'm going to pour the vowels into the consonants. Once mixed and heated at the proper temperature, the letters should yield an action that will be especially useful in this case."

Discover the "chemical
reaction" and look for it
on the map.

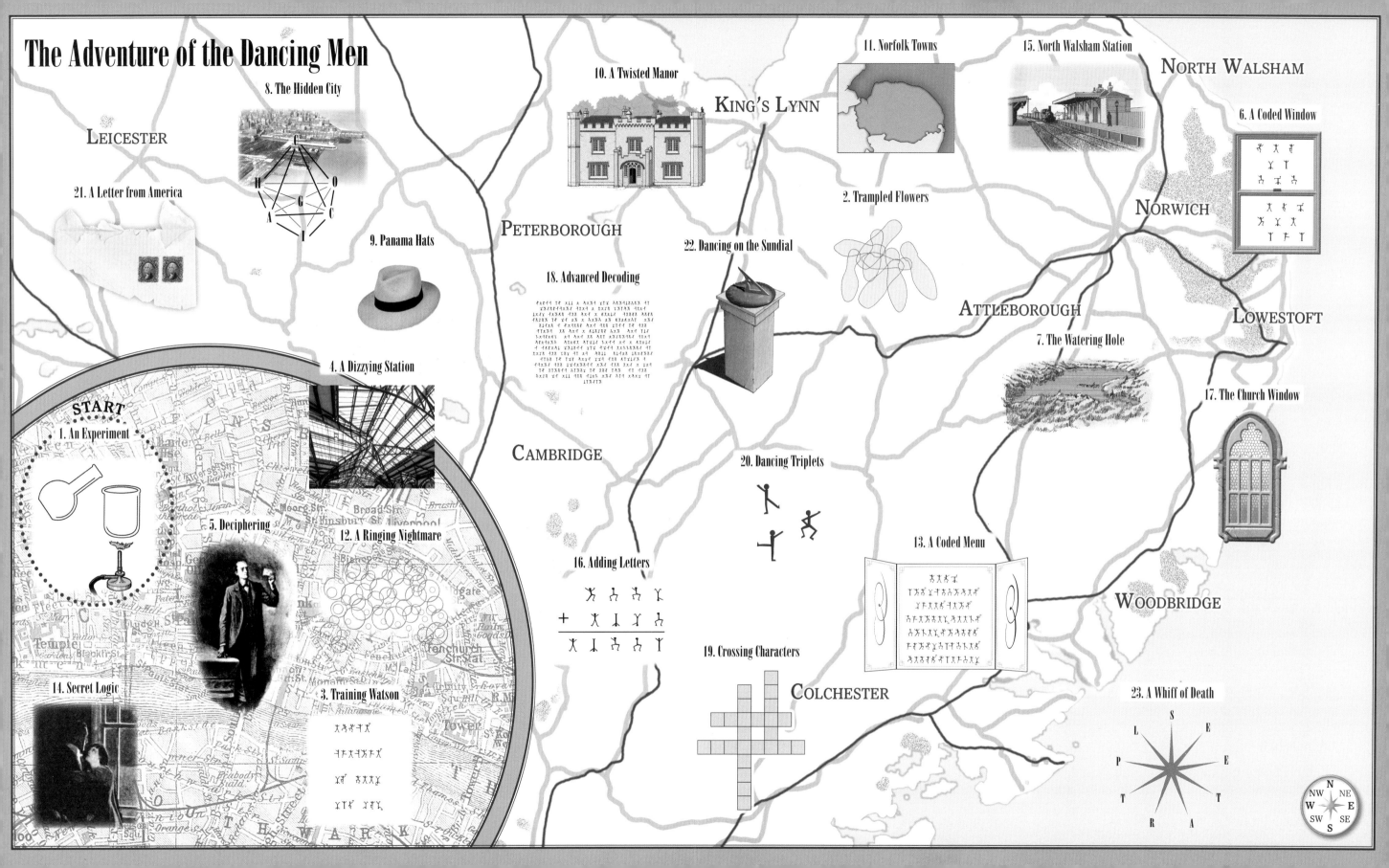

The Adventure of the Dancing Men

8. The Hidden City

10. A Twisted Manor

11. Norfolk Towns

15. North Walsham Station

NORTH WALSHAM

LEICESTER

KING'S LYNN

6. A Coded Window

NORWICH

21. A Letter from America

2. Trampled Flowers

9. Panama Hats

PETERBOROUGH

22. Dancing on the Sundial

18. Advanced Decoding

ATTLEBOROUGH

LOWESTOFT

7. The Watering Hole

4. A Dizzying Station

17. The Church Window

START

1. An Experiment

CAMBRIDGE

20. Dancing Triplets

5. Deciphering

12. A Ringing Nightmare

16. Adding Letters

13. A Coded Menu

WOODBRIDGE

14. Secret Logic

3. Training Watson

19. Crossing Characters

COLCHESTER

23. A Whiff of Death

✦ CHAPTER 2 ✦

The Adventure of the Dancing Men

MAP

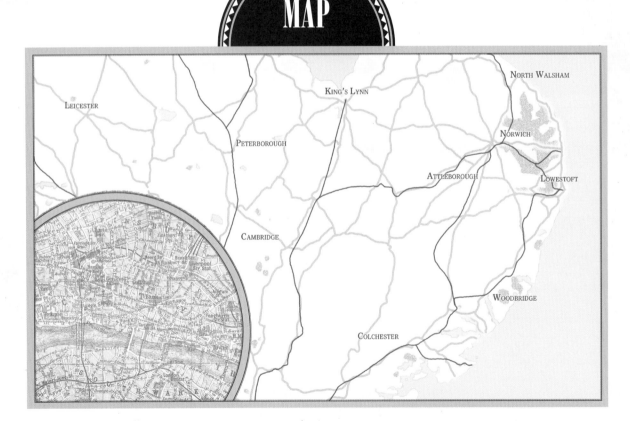

2
Trampled Flowers

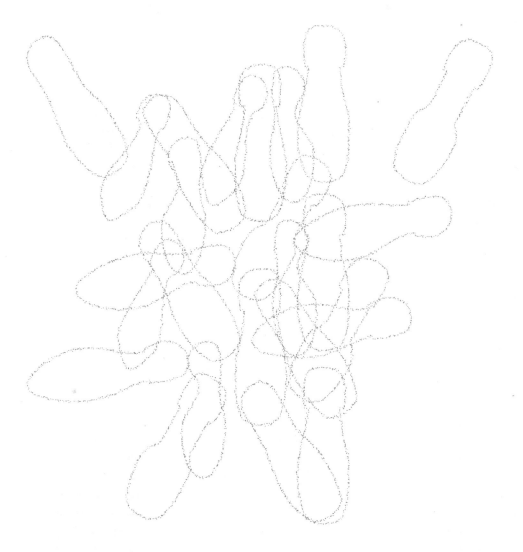

"Help me, Watson!" Holmes requests. "We must determine how many people passed the window by analyzing the footprints they left in the flower bed.

"How many different people trampled the flowers?"

> Look on the map for the coded window, overlooking the flower bed, and go there.

Training Watson

"Watson, I suggest you start memorizing this secret alphabet. A very ingenuous criminal created it hoping to disguise his messages behind childish-looking scribble. Each letter of the alphabet is represented by a figure of a dancing character. Notice that the flags held by some figures mark the end of the words.

"Working with a series of his documents, I managed to break the code: the column at the right gives the meaning of each figure. Now we'll be able to deceive the criminal using his own tool and send him a message that will precipitate his fall.

"Meanwhile, practice translating this message."

Look on the map for the resulting nightmare that is overwhelming Elsie.

A
B
C
D
E
F
G
H
I
J
K
L
M
N
O
P
Q
R
S
T
U
V
W
X
Y
Z

A Dizzying Station

"Mind your step but look at the roof," cautions Holmes. Each time I walk through this train station I wonder what the architects had in mind when they designed such a metallic maze. Did they intend to confuse the daily commuters? Personally, I cannot help but check to see if all the pieces are in their proper place.

"Can you count how many pieces are exchanged between the left- and right-hand sides of the roof?"

Find a much more traditional station on the map.

"We must interrupt the experiment," exclaims Holmes, "for our client has received a very strange document this morning with dancing figures drawn on a sheet of paper. It looks like the work of a child, but we must take it seriously, for the lives of several people appear to be at stake. We do not know enough to make anything of it yet, but we can start to analyze it.

"Notice that some characters are repeated. I propose we list the unique figures involved here, disregarding whether or not they hold flags."

> The number of different
> symbols used here, plus 1,
> tells you where you should
> go on the map.

A Coded Window

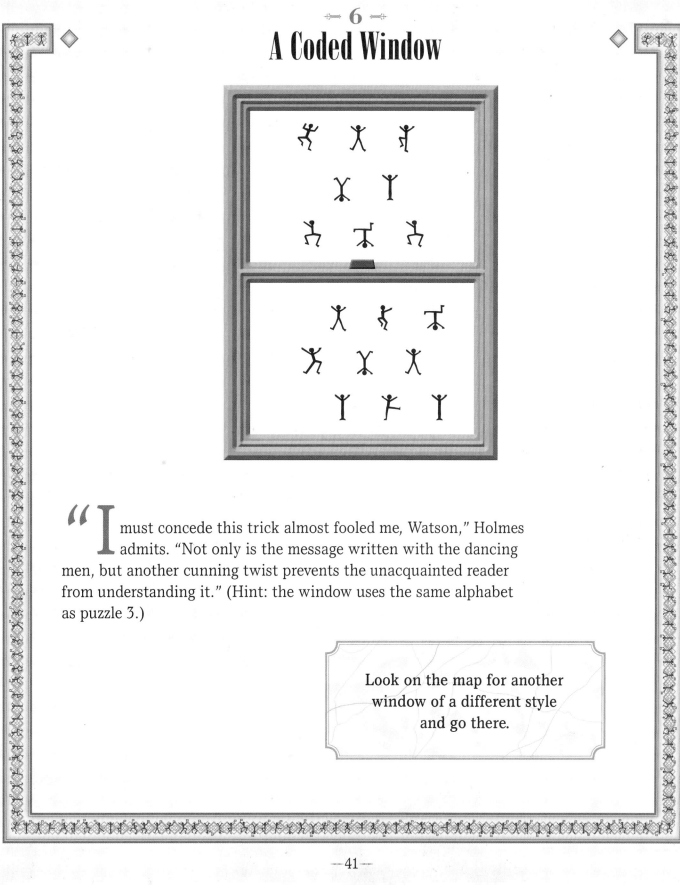

"I must concede this trick almost fooled me, Watson," Holmes admits. "Not only is the message written with the dancing men, but another cunning twist prevents the unacquainted reader from understanding it." (Hint: the window uses the same alphabet as puzzle 3.)

Look on the map for another window of a different style and go there.

— 7 —
The Watering Hole

PORPOISE   DEER

                                    VOLE

HEDGEHOG

                                        STOAT

                                    BAT

MUNTJAC

                                MINK

        FOX

"Aren't you fascinated by this watering hole near Riding Thorpe Manor?" Holmes asks Watson. "All the wild animals from the surrounding countryside need to share the water. Just imagine how careful some species must be to avoid meeting their predators, like criminals trying to avoid me!

"Beginning with PORPOISE and ending with STOAT, arrange the nine animals in a sequence so that animals that precede or follow each other do not share a common letter (for example, MINK—VOLE or FOX—DEER)."

> Find on the map a piece
> of clothing usually
> worn in the sun.

The Hidden City

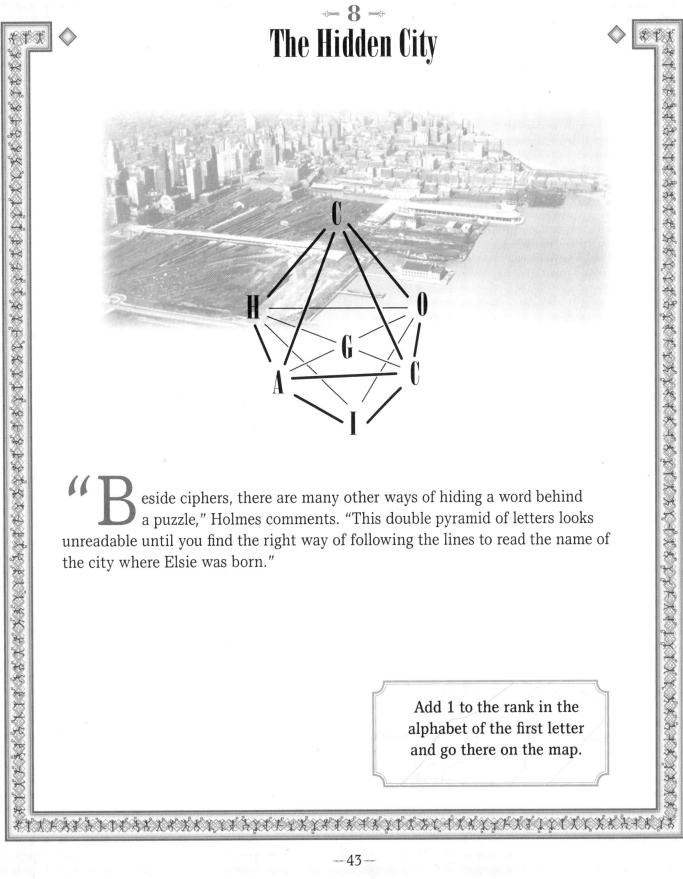

" **B**eside ciphers, there are many other ways of hiding a word behind a puzzle," Holmes comments. "This double pyramid of letters looks unreadable until you find the right way of following the lines to read the name of the city where Elsie was born."

Add 1 to the rank in the alphabet of the first letter and go there on the map.

Panama Hats

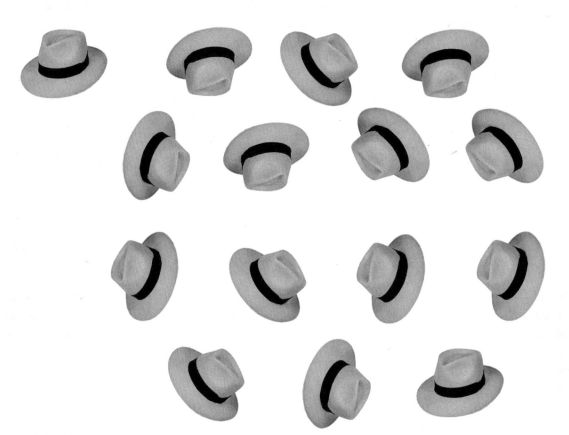

"The most arresting detail of our criminal's clothes, Watson, is that he wears a panama hat in Norfolk during the winter," Holmes explains. "Now, look at this drawing, where I sketched his hat several times; some are upright while others are rotated. Some are identical twins, the same as the original (on the top left) or with the same orientation, while others are triplets, each one with the same orientation as the original.

"How many triplets can you count?"

> The number of triplets, times 6, tells you where to go on the map.

A Twisted Manor

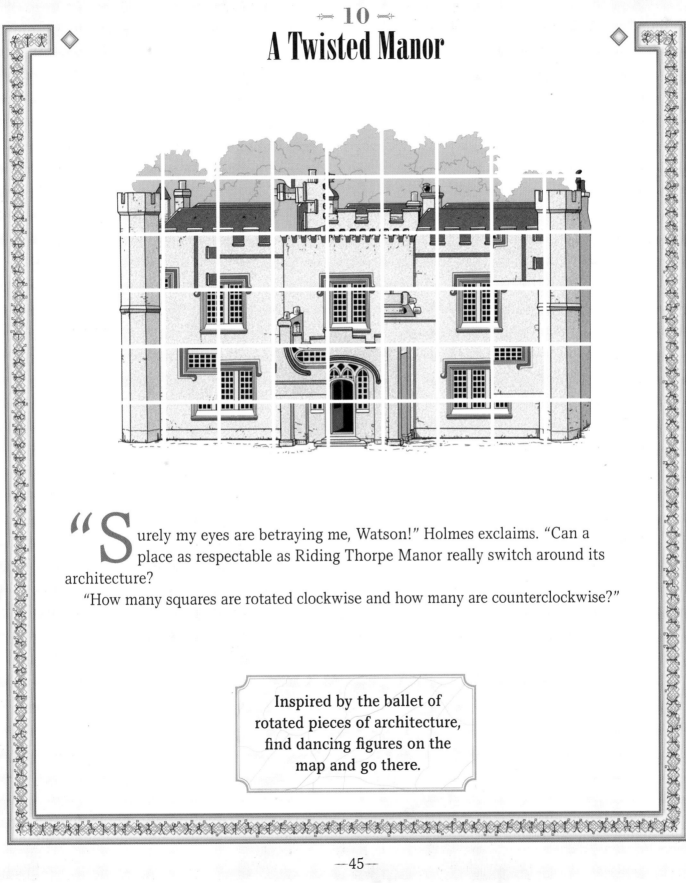

"Surely my eyes are betraying me, Watson!" Holmes exclaims. "Can a place as respectable as Riding Thorpe Manor really switch around its architecture?

"How many squares are rotated clockwise and how many are counterclockwise?"

Inspired by the ballet of rotated pieces of architecture, find dancing figures on the map and go there.

Norfolk Towns

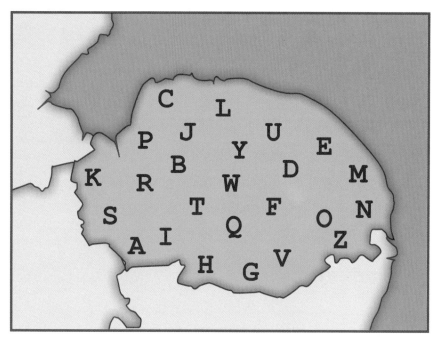

NORWICH

CROMER

HOLT

SHERINGHAM

AYLSHAM

HUNSTANTON

FALKENHAM

WHYMONDHAM

DEREHAM

BLAKENEY

WROXHAM

SWAFFHAM

WATTON

"If we were not so deeply involved in this adventure, we could visit many interesting places around here in Norfolk County," Holmes wonders out loud, "especially these thirteen towns I have listed.

"Can you tell which one of these places cannot be spelled out using the twenty-five letters on the county map (possibly using some letters twice or more), Watson?"

Look for a nearby
manor on the map
and go there.

12
A Ringing Nightmare

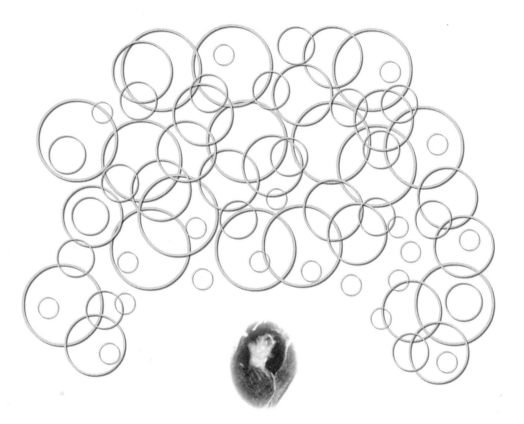

"Based on the information my friend Wilson Hargreave of the New York Police Bureau sent me, I'm sure poor Elsie's nightmares are about her fateful engagement to Abe Slaney when she was growing up in America. I imagine her overwhelmed by visions of rings like the one she should never have accepted from Abe. But what troubles me most is that there is something wrong with the number of different-sized rings.

"How many sizes and how many rings of each size can you count, Watson?"

Go to the object on the map that
arrived from Elsie's birthplace.

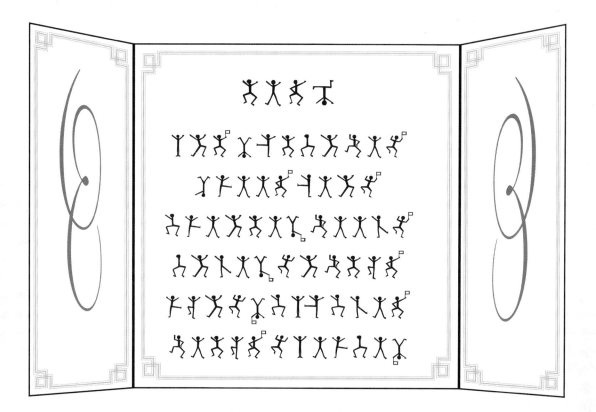

"**M**ark my word, Watson. Those dancing men and the associated events will impress local minds so deeply that it won't be long before even the inn keepers write and post their menus in the secret writing," Holmes promises.

"Can you put your code training to use here, Watson?" (Hint: the menu uses the same alphabet as puzzle 3; remember that flags signal ends of words.)

Look on the map for a crossword
of the main characters involved
and go there.

"Let's try some logic problems, Watson, to get our minds working. One problem in this case is that our client swore to respect his wife's secrets. He won't question her about her former life or about the mysterious events that have been troubling her for several months. He may not be aware that secrets have their own, unique logic. Just as I deduced that you did not invest in goldfields with your friend Thurston, let's apply some assumptions to this case. We know:

(1) Blue-eyed people wearing hats can be trusted to keep a secret.
(2) All angry golf players have blue eyes.
(3) Everybody, sometimes, wears a hat.
(4) All country squires play golf.

Since our client is a country squire and sometimes gets angry, what can his wife do to make sure she can trust him with a secret? Following the assumptions above, can you apply logic and answer the question correctly?"

Look on the map for Watson's training in deciphering.

"Let's not be fooled by this broken view of North Walsham station, Watson! Even though assembling its nine pieces seems simple enough, it cannot be done. There's no logic to it.

"Do you see why?"

Look for the surrounding
towns on the map.

Adding Letters

"I pity criminals sometimes, Watson," Holmes admits. "Being of an evil nature and illogical, they have missed a very interesting, and logical, way of using their dancing men code. Here, I have written down a sum where the numbers from 0 to 9 are replaced by symbols. For example, the second symbol in the first row, the last one in the second row, and the fourth in the third row represent the same number.

"If you apply the correct logic, you'll find there is only one way to replace the symbols with numbers and get a correct result."

> Look for a venerable instrument
> in the garden that will tell you the
> time and go there on the map.

The Church Window

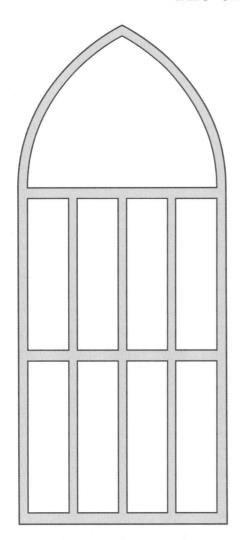

"The church's window arrangement of glass panels suggests a number problem, simple yet challenging, Watson. There are 9 areas, which consist of 8 panes and the top.

"How can you place the numbers 1 to 9 in each separate area without the numbers touching their neighbors in any direction (for example, 8 cannot touch a 9 or 7; and 4 cannot touch a 5 or 3, etc.)?" (Hint: there are a couple of solutions.)

Find on the map a restaurant menu written with the dancing figures and go there.

Advance Decoding

[A coded message in dancing men figures spanning the top portion of the page]

"**W**atson, we may have to solve other coded messages in future cases," Holmes warns. "I suggest you do not leave this adventure without a genuine experience of actually breaking an unknown code. Here is the confession of the villain, coded with the familiar dancing men but arranged as a key to correspond with the Latin alphabet rather than the key used in puzzle 3 to train you.

"Let me remind you of the basics of deciphering: it relies on letter frequency. E is by far the most frequent letter in English, and the other common letters are A, N, R, S, T, and I—although not necessarily in that order."

Find on the map a reference to scent, an unavoidable clue for a professional sleuth.

Crossing Characters

"Names apparently have their own logic, Watson. Among the five people we have met in this adventure, only four can crisscross harmoniously on the grid. And you shouldn't be surprised when you discover the odd one out."

MARTIN

HARGREAVE

CUBITT

THURSTON

SLANEY

Count the letters of the odd person out, add 10, and go there on the map.

Dancing Triplets

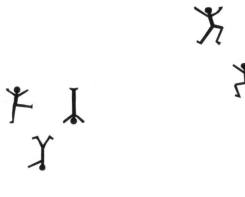

"Logic can reside anywhere, Watson," Holmes reminds. "Look closely at these five triplets of symbols.

"Which triplet is logically different from the four others?"

Find on the map a place where these dancers could have left their footprints.

A Letter from America

"The stamp on this letter betrays its origin, since it features an American president instead of a British queen. However, if the sender wished to be playful, he could have rotated one of the stamps before attaching it to the envelope.

"The five groupings below do not show all of the possibilities. Can you draw the missing one, Watson?"

Go to a foreign city hidden
behind its own letters on
the map.

" **H**ow strange!" shouts Holmes. "Every possible surface has been used to write these dancing figures. Do you see that message scribbled on the pedestal of the sundial?

"Your knowledge of the dansing men from puzzle 3 will be useful here, Watson."

The message clearly
tells you where to go
next on the map.

A Whiff of Death

"A trained eye and a good magnifying glass are not always sufficient to solve a case, Watson," Holmes lectures. In this case one needed a sensitive nose to identify the smell of gunpowder, which was essential in determining who fired first and who the real murderer was.

"This brings us back to our chemical experiment before we started the case. The basic ingredient of gunpowder is potassium nitrate, and you can read its traditional name on the points of the star by jumping over a fixed number of letters."

> Figure out the name of the
> component to conclude the
> adventure and then read the
> next page.

Chapter Clue

"Did you notice a tiny but strange mistake in this chapter, Watson? Ah, of course, you couldn't see it because your mind is not trained to notice the small discrepancies that I, as a detective, call clues. These details, generally unheeded by ordinary mortals, are the essential stones on which I build my solutions to the mysteries."

The anomaly you found in this chapter is a clue to the final word puzzle. Make a note of the letter and save it below to solve the puzzle on page 163, after you have gone through the six adventures in the book.

Clue for chapter 2: _____

CHAPTER 3

A Scandal in Bohemia

I n this next adventure, Holmes immediately tells his client that he doesn't need to wear a mask, as he already knows the disguised man's identity, the King of Bohemia. Too many obvious clues point to his name, country, and rank. Many nobility, and even monarchs, are standard clients at 221B Baker Street, and Holmes treats each one with respect—without ever letting himself be impressed by their social status, as if somehow their rank was more of a handicap than an advantage in life. He takes pride in helping them with the greatest discretion to preserve their dignity. As Watson often points out, many accounts of Holmes's adventures will never be released for fear they might compromise well-known heads of states and high society. Due to his Victorian morals, Holmes doesn't hesitate to break the law now and then to avoid potential scandals for his royal clients. Worse still, the woman Holmes fails to burglarize makes fun of him and he forever remembers her as one of the brightest minds he has ever encountered.

As explained in the introduction, tear out the map attached to this chapter and keep it with you as a travel guide. It will be essential for steering you through the strange places and events within this chapter.

Start with the first puzzle on the next page, solve it, and then follow the boxed hint to find the next puzzle number on the map. With the puzzle's number above the title, go to the corresponding puzzle in the chapter.

Repeat this sequence with each puzzle, going back and forth from the puzzles to the map and back again, until you reach the last case.

Breaking Holmes's Pipe

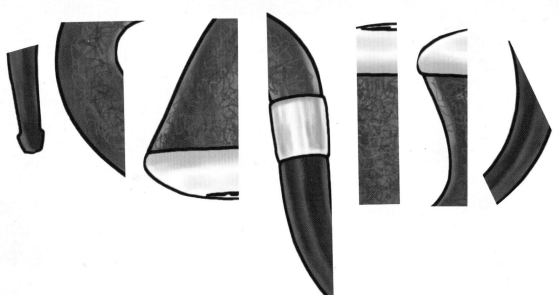

"**I**'m so sorry, Holmes! I understand you are smoking cigars because you've broken your best pipe, the one made of meerschaum and calabash, and imported from Tasmania."

"It was only an object, Watson, with no feelings of its own, hence no need for mine. Yet I do wish to remember this important item in my life, so I've drawn a sketch of the pieces as they lay broken on the floor."

"You're making fun of me, Holmes. That simply can't be an accurate sketch of the broken pieces."

"Excellent, Watson. Thanks to my company, you are making impressive progress. Which piece does not match?"

Locate Holmes's smoke
rings on the map.

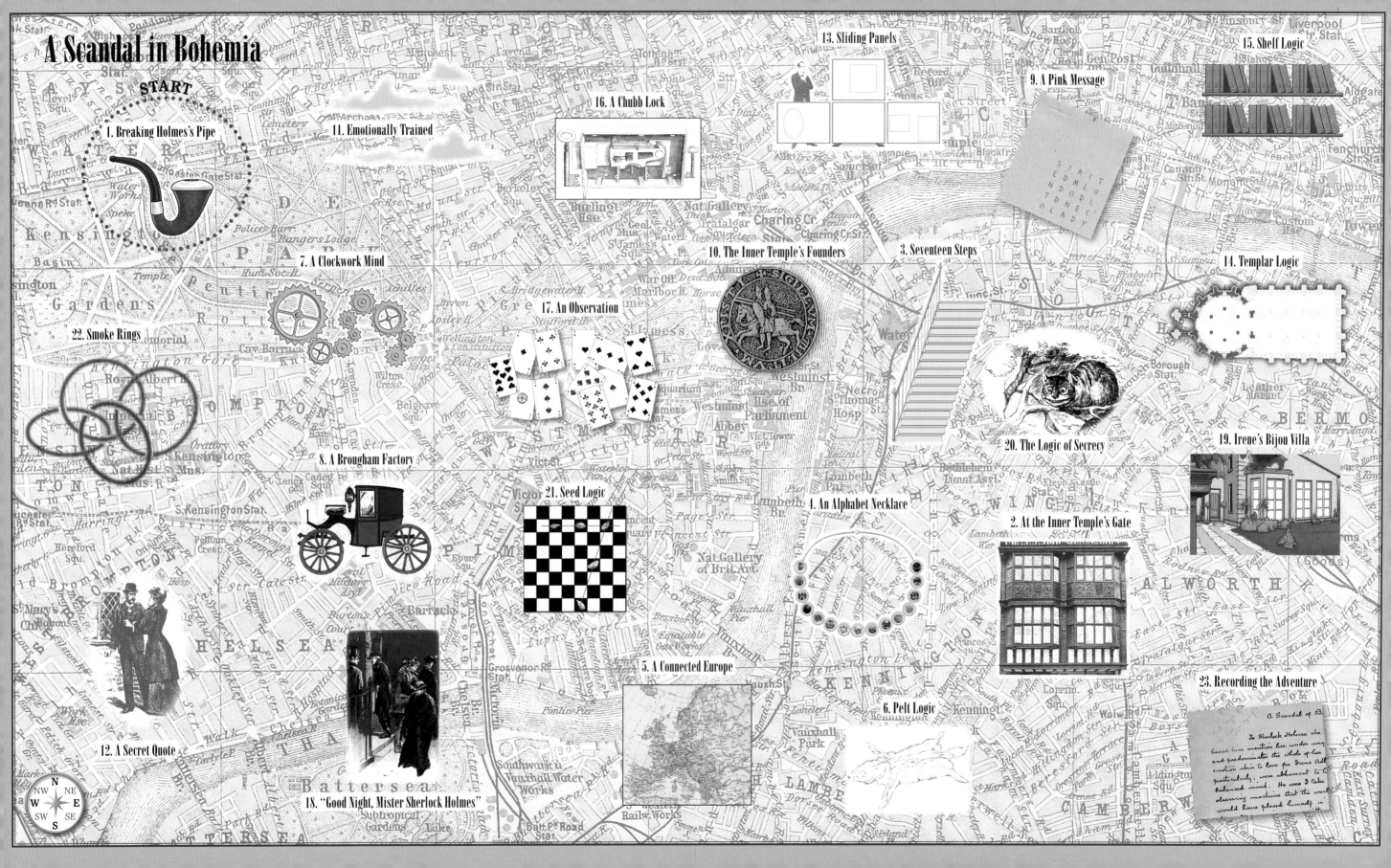

A Scandal in Bohemia

START

1. Breaking Holmes's Pipe

11. Emotionally Trained

13. Sliding Panels

9. A Pink Message

15. Shelf Logic

16. A Chubb Lock

7. A Clockwork Mind

10. The Inner Temple's Founders

3. Seventeen Steps

14. Templar Logic

22. Smoke Rings

17. An Observation

20. The Logic of Secrecy

19. Irene's Bijou Villa

8. A Brougham Factory

21. Seed Logic

4. An Alphabet Necklace

2. At the Inner Temple's Gate

12. A Secret Quote

5. A Connected Europe

6. Pelt Logic

23. Recording the Adventure

18. "Good Night, Mister Sherlock Holmes"

CHAPTER 3

A Scandal in Bohemia

MAP

At the Inner Temple's Gate

"Look, Watson!" Holmes points out. "Our Mr. Godfrey Norton, a lawyer in the Inner Temple, left his office in a hurry and barely had time to improvise a secret message on the window panes for his clients.

"However, he left enough clues to allow the content to be easily read without openly revealing his private business."

The message contains a first and last name. The sum of letters indicates where to go on the map.

Seventeen Steps

"Most people waste valuable time while climbing a staircase, missing a great opportunity to train their minds. They mechanically count the steps. Whenever I climb the seventeen steps to my chambers, I imagine a fixed logical sequence displayed on the steps.

"Can you figure out the logic at play, Watson? Do you see which number is wrong? Keep in mind, though, that more than one pattern can be involved.

"Here is a clue: the wrong number should be a square."

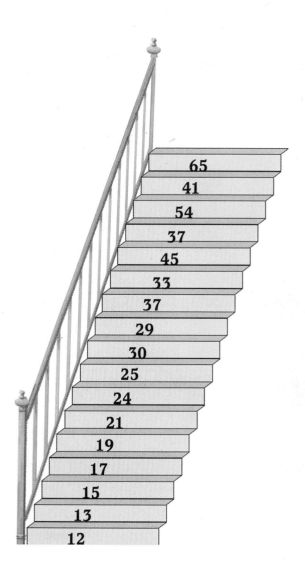

Go to a mystery square of letters on the map.

An Alphabet Necklace

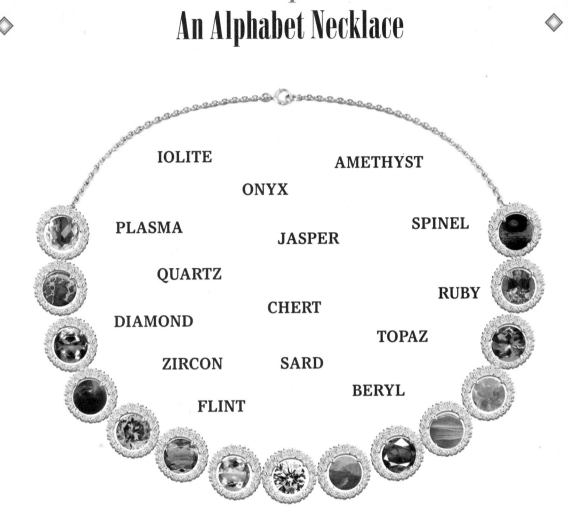

IOLITE AMETHYST

ONYX

PLASMA SPINEL

JASPER

QUARTZ RUBY

CHERT

DIAMOND TOPAZ

ZIRCON SARD

BERYL

FLINT

"Here's a fun game to get your mind working," Holmes challenges Watson. "Imagine you are stringing a necklace with these fifteen different gemstones, ranging from AMETHYST to IOLITE. To enhance the quality of this piece of jewelry, carefully avoid any contact between stones sharing common letters."

Find another natural form of apparel trimming on the map.

LONDON	CARLSBAD	CASSEL-FALSTEIN	DARLINGTON
EGLONITZ	EGLOW	EGRIA	ODESSA
PRAGUE	WARSAW	BOHEMIA	HOLLAND

"AAlthough this case takes place in London, more distant plages are involved. They can easily be joined with six horizontal and vertical lines as on the grid below.

"However, I know you can join them even better, Watson, with only five straight lines and closing the circuit by ending on your starting point."

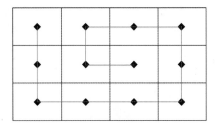

Go to Watson's manuscript on the map.

Pelt Logic

ASTRAKHAN

WOLF

KARAKUL

ERMINE

CHINCHILLA

COYOTE

SEAL

OTTER

FOX

MINK

POSSUM

RABBIT

MARTEN

RACCOON

SABLE

SKUNK

BEAVER

"Consider this set of pelt names, Watson. There is an interesting, logical subset of six pelts among them that include: FOX, WOLF, MINK, SABLE, and SEAL.

"Can you work out the logic that defines this subset and deduce the sixth special item?"

The rank in the alphabet of the first letter of the sixth pelt tells you where to go on the map.

"My mind is a perfect reasoning machine, Watson. I've trained it to function as precisely as a clockwork.

"For instance, in the gear mechanisms above, can you figure out the effect of the large gear on the top left on the small one on the bottom right? When the large gear rotates full circle, how many revolutions does the last gear make?"

Proceed to another
logic problem on
the map featuring
playing cards.

A Brougham Factory

"Did you see our client's brougham and the two beauties drawing it? What a perfect vehicle—both elegant and efficient! Can you think of a better and more logical way of getting around in a modern city, Watson?

"How many complete broughams can be assembled with the parts displayed on this page?"

Go to the number of complete broughams on the map.

A Pink Message

"Watson, did you notice that private message that was scribbled in a corner on the back of the pink sheet of paper and then poorly erased? I wonder if it was the first draft of a diplomatic message that was later sent by the King of Bohemia?

"Can you read it by starting at a corner and following contiguous letters?"

The number of letters of
the longest word in the
message shows where to go
next on the map.

The Inner Temple's Founders

"Did you know, Watson, that the Inner Temple is far more venerable than it looks? It was founded more than eight centuries ago. The founders were hardly lawyers, like the present occupants.

"Can you read who they were by starting on a letter and then keep skipping over the same number of letters around the seal?"

Go to the sacred map
of the Temple Church
on the map.

Emotionally Trained

"When you train your mind as I do, Watson, to be a precise and logical tool, the first thing to learn is how to master your emotions. I adhere to the list below compiled by my ancient colleague Aristotle. Although he rarely focused his attention on crime, his works remain useful as a basic reference. This grid is a good place to practice your knowledge of emotions.

"Each word on the list can be found twice, either horizontally or vertically or backwards—except for one of them."

```
A  S  H  A  M  E  E  S  I  R  P  R  U  S  P       FEAR
S  B  P  C  D  E  S  A  D  N  E  S  S  F  I       ANGER
A  L  R  G  I  J  O  N  P  F  N  Y  N  L  T       SADNESS
D  O  I  F  S  O  R  G  I  E  V  T  J  O  S       JOY
N  V  D  E  M  Y  R  E  T  A  Y  I  E  V  H       DISGUST
E  E  E  A  N  G  E  R  Y  R  G  P  I  E  A       PITY
S  N  K  R  E  P  D  I  S  G  U  S  T  S  M       CONTEMPT
S  E  T  P  M  E  T  N  O  C  S  H  A  M  E       SURPRISE
E  S  I  R  P  R  U  S  S  T  E  D  I  R  P       ENVY
Y  O  J  S  T  S  U  G  S  I  D  I  D  N  I       LOVE
I  N  D  I  G  N  A  T  I  O  N  Y  V  N  E       SHAME
                                                  PRIDE
                                                  INDIGNATION
```

The rank in the list of the missing emotion tells you the next step on the map.

A Secret Quote

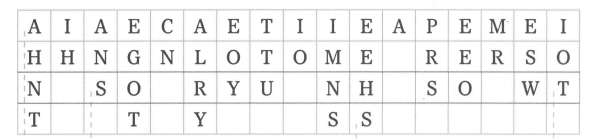

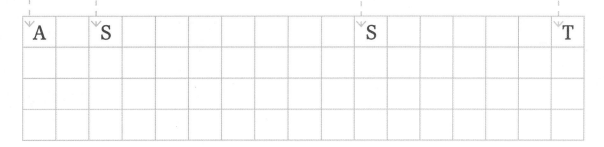

A	I	A	E	C	A	E	T	I	I	E	A	P	E	M	E	I
H	H	N	G	N	L	O	T	O	M	E		R	E	R	S	O
N		S	O		R	Y	U		N	H		S	O		W	T
T			T		Y				S	S						

A		S						S								T

"The key theme in this adventure, Watson, is 'secret' of the utmost importance for one's personal privacy. It should not be taken lightly.

"Let's make an exception, though, and play around with it. Display a humorous comment about secrecy in the empty squares below by dropping each letter from the squares above into a correct square below."

Go to an apparatus designed to help keep secrets mechanically on the map.

Sliding Panels

"Irene Adler hid the scandalous letter in a recess of a complex piece of furniture designed to contain up to four different pictures. Three sliding panels can hold photographs of different formats.

"Aside from the pictures themselves, and considering only the empty frames, can you tell how many different individual areas are defined within the main frame when the three panels are centered into position, Watson?"

> Count the number of
> areas, multiply by 2, and
> go there on the map.

Templar Logic

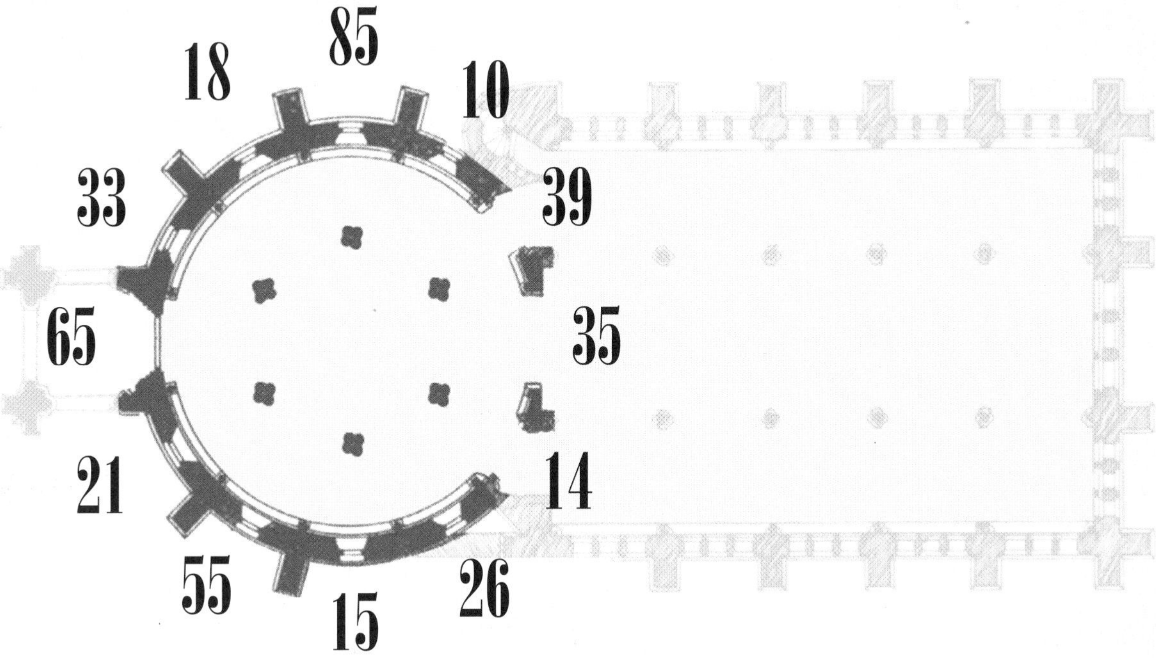

85

18

10

33

39

65

35

21

14

55

26

15

"The most ancient part of the Inner Temple, of course, is the Temple Church, designed by the Templars with a circular nave similar to the original Church of the Holy Sepulchre in Jerusalem.

"I like to imagine this nave as a 'temple of logic' as well. The numbers posted on the twelve openings attempt to follow a logic pattern. All but one number manage it. Is the logic obvious to you, Watson?"

Go to the odd
number out on
the map.

"I'm sorry, Watson, but I'm wondering what you'll think of me today. From a logical point of view, my bookshelves are untidy, or didn't you notice the problem?"

Go on and locate more
logic on the map involving
a staircase.

A Chubb Lock

"A Chubb lock secures the door of Irene Adler's villa. I admire the mechanical and logical mind of its inventor, Jeremiah Chubb. Not only does the lock alert the owner of a thief's unsuccessful attempt to open it, but it also withstood countless tries for over thirty years.

"The main parts of the lock are the BAR, CASE, COVER, CURTAIN, CYLINDER, DETECTOR, KEY, LEVER, LOCK, REGULATOR, SCREWS, SPRINGS, STUMP, TALON, and TUMBLER, and they all fit in the crossword below. I must find another way of getting into the premises quickly before her fiancé returns from his office at the Inner Temple."

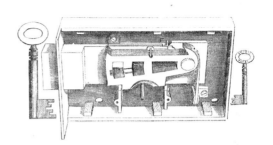

Head to the first place mentioned here by Sherlock Holmes on the map.

An Observation

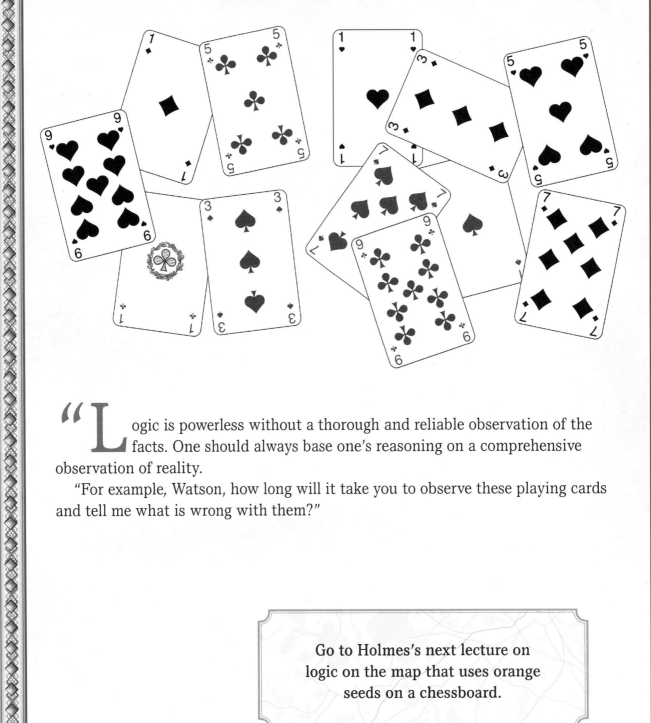

"Logic is powerless without a thorough and reliable observation of the facts. One should always base one's reasoning on a comprehensive observation of reality.

"For example, Watson, how long will it take you to observe these playing cards and tell me what is wrong with them?"

Go to Holmes's next lecture on logic on the map that uses orange seeds on a chessboard.

"Good Night, Mister Sherlock Holmes"

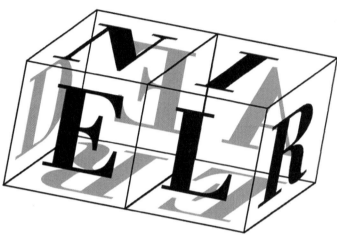

"D o not include this in your account of the case, Watson, but I must confess I'm touched by this woman's attention. As she passed by, surprisingly saying 'Good night, Mister Sherlock Holmes,' she slipped into my pocket two glass cubes engraved with her name.

"The words can be read by following their contiguous faces. Yet, she was in such a hurry that she didn't realize there are flaws in the etching, which is an endearing and telling clue as to her emotions about me."

Go to Europe on the map.

Irene's Bijou Villa

"Watson, even though we are not inside the villa to hear precisely what Godfrey Norton is saying to Irene Adler, we can distinguish some of their words through the windows.

"Can you guess at least one word that mentions a place?"

Go to the gate of the
place mentioned in the
message on the map.

The Logic of Secrecy

"Concerning secrets, I think of my esteemed and logical, albeit playful, colleague Lewis Carroll.

"I wonder if he would have feared that his Cheshire Cat could betray a secret, using logic and the assumptions below, conveniently reorganized."

NO CREATURE EVER SMILES THAT IS NOT COMPASSIONATE.

ONLY LOOSE LIPS BREAK A CONFIDENCE.

CHESHIRE CATS SMILE NATURALLY.

COMPASSION GENERATES RESPECT.

ALL SECRETS ARE CONFIDENTIAL.

RESPECT PRECLUDES INCONSIDERATE TALKING.

Go to the quote on the matter on the map.

Seed Logic

"Now, Watson, facts are important, but logic is essential to organize them and develop hypotheses. Suppose these five orange seeds are basic observations that I have collected and placed on a chessboard representing a case. In addition, suppose you need to align three of them to formulate a hypothesis. From the way I've placed the five seeds, I have only two alignments and hence only draw two hypotheses.

"This is where creativity comes in, and you need to be more than just a basic logician. There are ways of organizing the five seeds on the chessboard so that they display more alignments of three seeds, hence draw more hypotheses. How many alignments of three seeds can you get in one display?"

Go exercise your logic with
bookshelves on the map.

Smoke Rings

"Y ou amaze me, Holmes," Watson exclaims. "Even while smoking, you keep studying logical problems. Although evanescent smoke rings are the very image of the futility of a mind dominated by emotions, are they following a specific pattern here?

"I wonder if the four rings can freely float away by themselves. Are the four smoke rings independent from one another?"

Locate a display of emotions
on the map.

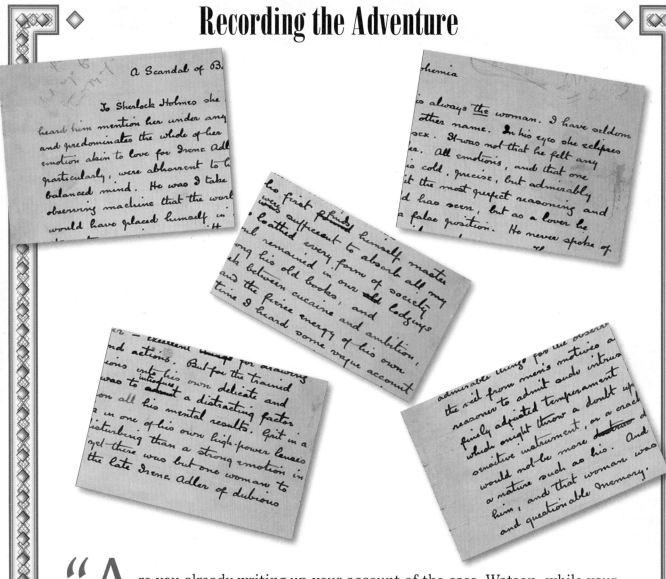

"Are you already writing up your account of the case, Watson, while your memory is still fresh?" Holmes asks. "Wouldn't it sound better if you titled it 'A Scandal *in* Bohemia' instead of 'A Scandal *of* Bohemia'? I do not mind your mentioning how much Irene Adler impressed me, as I will never forget her brilliant mind!

"However, one part of your manuscript doesn't fit with the other four. Which one?"

From the original manuscript of Sir Arthur Conan Doyle. Photo courtesy of
The Arthur Conan Doyle Encyclopedia (www.arthur-conan-doyle.com).

Go to the next page.

Chapter Clue

"Did you notice a tiny but strange mistake in this chapter, Watson? Ah, of course, you couldn't see it because your mind is not trained to notice the small discrepancies that I, as a detective, call clues. These details, generally unheeded by ordinary mortals, are the essential stones on which I build my solutions to the mysteries."

The anomaly you found in this chapter is a clue to the final word puzzle. Make a note of the letter and save it below to solve the puzzle on page 163, after you have gone through the six adventures in the book.

Clue for chapter 3: _____

CHAPTER 4
The Hound of the Baskervilles

A sleuth on the scent of a vicious hound, Detective Holmes encounters old legends of supernatural horrors with his signature calm and unwavering logic, but the gloomy setting only exacerbates the dangerous situation. Baskerville Hall lies within the rugged and sometimes treacherous moors, where escaped convicts, horrendous beasts, rare insects, ancient monuments, and cold-hearted, conniving criminals are slyly sneaking around.

Like following a narrow track through a mire, step carefully through the puzzles inspired by the novel *The Hound of the Baskervilles*. Trust your logic, as Holmes trusts his keen sense of smell, to hunt down the villains.

As explained in the introduction, tear out the map attached to this chapter and keep it with you as a travel guide. It will be essential for steering you through the strange places and events within this chapter.

Start with the first puzzle on the next page, solve it, and then follow the boxed hint to find the next puzzle number on the map. With the puzzle's number above the title, go to the corresponding puzzle in the chapter.

Repeat this sequence with each puzzle, going back and forth from the puzzles to the map and back again, until you reach the last case.

Sticking to Logic

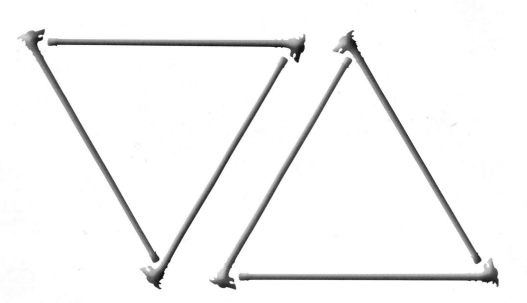

"Watson, I'd like to test your ingenuity by using the walking stick that our new client left behind yesterday," Holmes remarks. "In detective work, our minds often need to break away from ordinary reasoning and dive into deep realms of analytical thought that are quite out of reach for the mere mortal.

"Let's imagine you have six such walking sticks. How would you place them to make just four identical triangles?"

Look on the map for a skull.

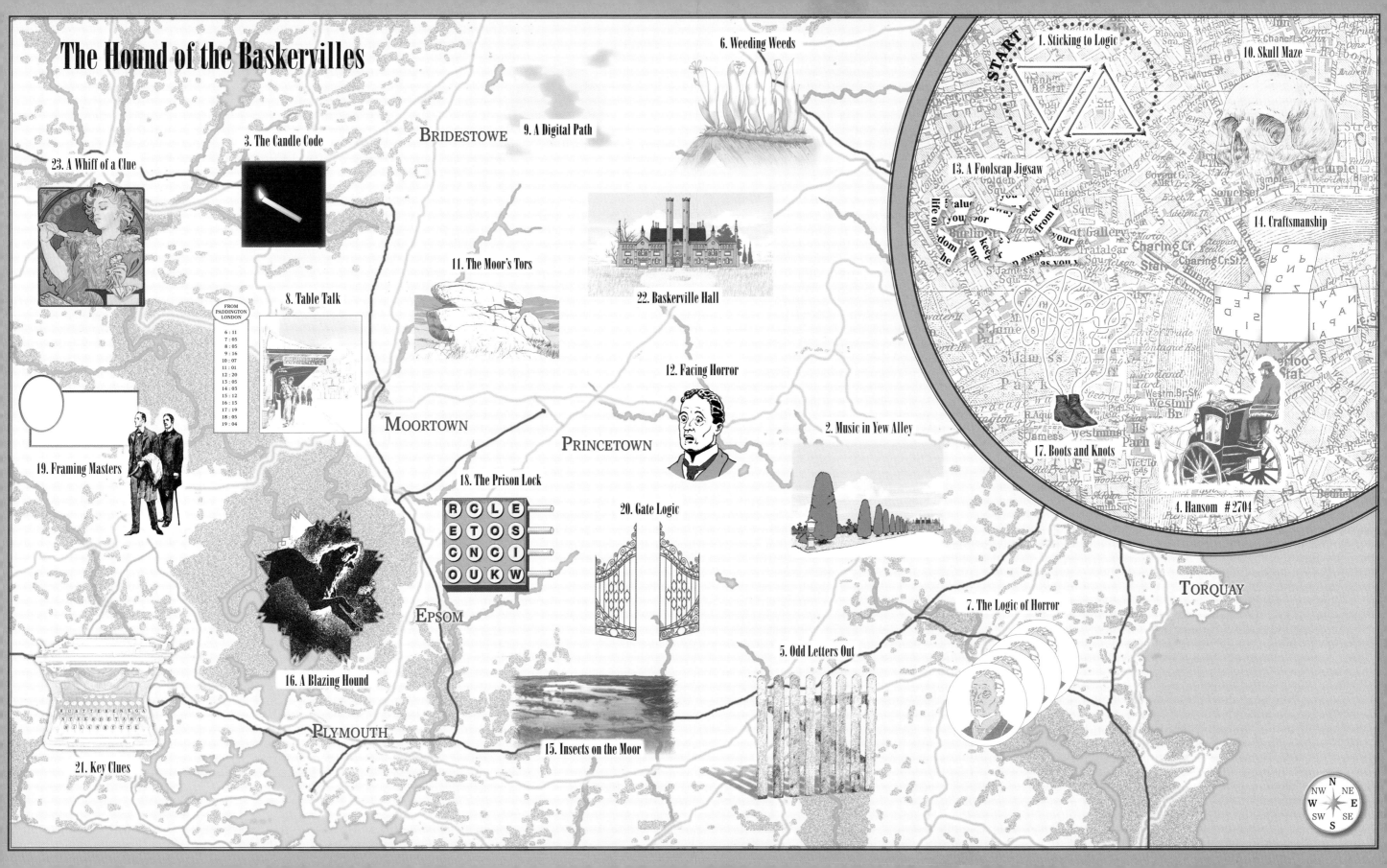

The Hound of the Baskervilles

1. Sticking to Logic
6. Weeding Weeds
10. Skull Maze
9. A Digital Path
BRIDESTOWE
13. A Foolscap Jigsaw
3. The Candle Code
23. A Whiff of a Clue
14. Craftsmanship
11. The Moor's Tors
22. Baskerville Hall
8. Table Talk

FROM
PADDINGTON
LONDON

6 : 11
7 : 05
8 : 05
9 : 16
10 : 07
11 : 01
12 : 20
13 : 05
14 : 03
15 : 12
16 : 15
17 : 19
18 : 05
19 : 04

12. Facing Horror
MOORTOWN
2. Music in Yew Alley
19. Framing Masters
17. Boots and Knots
PRINCETOWN
4. Hansom #2704
18. The Prison Lock
20. Gate Logic
7. The Logic of Horror
EPSOM
TORQUAY
5. Odd Letters Out
16. A Blazing Hound
PLYMOUTH
21. Key Clues
15. Insects on the Moor

NW N NE
W E
SW S SE

⊰ CHAPTER 4 ⊱

The Hound of the Baskervilles

MAP

FROM
PADDINGTON
LONDON

6 : 11
7 : 05
8 : 05
9 : 16
10 : 07
11 : 01
12 : 20
13 : 05
14 : 03
15 : 12
16 : 15
17 : 19
18 : 05
19 : 04

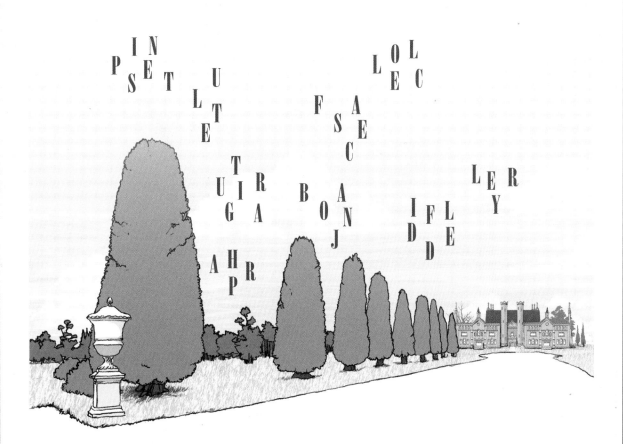

"Due to its elasticity, yew wood was Britain's main, raw material when wooden bows and arrows preceded rifles and cannons," Holmes explains. "Later, the wood's elastic trait was put to a more peaceful use to make musical instruments, which I currently envision as playing all around us while we walk down the famous Yew Alley of Baskerville Hall.

"Only one word is not an instrument and hints at our next step."

Find the one word unrelated to music and go to it on the map.

The Candle Code

"I'm afraid you'll have to rewrite your account of this adventure, Watson, as we've been fooled by the butler, Mr. Barrymore! I don't believe for a second that he was just checking to see if the windows were locked. He was using the candle to shine some type of message. Notice he was using two candles, since a single flame is too weak to illuminate anything from a distance.

"Clearly, Barrymore was sending a signal to his brother-in-law, the convict, hiding out on the moor! Can you decipher his system?" (Hint: As Sherlock Holmes is fond of saying, "Time is of the essence.")

Go to a more modern message-writing device on the map.

Hansom #2704

"A remarkable number, this 2704, Watson, and easily memorized. Just remember you can arrive at it by simply inserting one or several arithmetic symbols between the nine digits below.

"How many math symbols do you need, not counting the parentheses?"

$$3 \quad 9 \quad 2 \quad 5 \quad 4 \quad 7 \quad 1 \quad 8 \quad 6 = 2704$$

Head to the masters at the art gallery on the map.

Odd Letters Out

"Someone painted the names of local trees on the planks of the wicket-gate but got one letter wrong in each tree name.

"Can you still read all the names, Watson?"

Examine the map for the
last tree in alphabetical
order and head there.

Weeding Weeds

"Here is an interesting aesthetic choice, Watson. In the hamlet of Grimpen, homeowners let weeds grow on top of their thatched roofs. It makes for a wild weed patch above their houses.

"Unfortunately, the weeds need weeding, as unwanted letters have crept into the weeds' names! Can you form a word with these letters?"

> The word formed with
> unwanted letters tells you
> where to head next on the map.

The Logic of Horror

THE UNBEARABLE CAUSES PANIC.

❅

HORROR IS UNBEARABLE.

❅

NO FEELING OF DANGER WITHOUT A PERCEPTION OF THREATS.

❅

THREATS ONLY EXIST THROUGH AN AWARENESS OF CONSEQUENCES.

❅

ONE NEEDS IMAGINATION TO BE AWARE OF CONSEQUENCES.

❅

NO PANIC WITHOUT FEAR.

❅

FEAR ONLY DEVELOPS THROUGH CONSCIOUSNESS OF DANGER.

"Horror is definitely an essential element in this case. The villain obviously used it as a weapon to kill Sir Charles Baskerville. That said, Watson, I wonder if such a scheme would have worked on a victim lacking imagination.

"Using the assumptions above and logic, if the late Sir Charles had been without this faculty, would he have survived his horrific encounter at the wicket-gate?"

Look for the mansion on the map where our horror story began.

FROM LONDON PADDINGTON STATION
6 : 11
7 : 05
8 : 05
9 : 16
10 : 07
11 : 01
12 : 20
13 : 05
14 : 03
15 : 12
16 : 15
17 : 19
18 : 05
19 : 04

"How can anyone ever get bored in a train station, Watson? You can exercise your mind and pass the time by simply analyzing the timetables. Especially now, while waiting for Inspector Lestrade to arrive from London Paddington Station! Do you see how the station is sending us a coded warning message through the arrival minutes?

"Can you decipher it, or do you need my help?"

Go to the place hidden in the message on the map.

A Digital Path

1	7	5	8	3	7	9	8	1	5	3	1	8	1	2	3
9	5	6	3	9	3	4	6	2	7	2	5	4	3	7	6
1	3	5	7	7	9	2	8	5	4	8	6	2	7	3	4
9	7	1	6	4	2	3	5	4	2	3	7	6	1	6	3
2	4	5	8	2	3	4	8	2	5	4	6	4	3	5	2
4	9	1	4	5	9	3	2	9	4	1	2	7	1	2	7
6	7	6	3	7	2	1	8	7	9	5	6	2	3	4	5
5	4	5	7	9	4	3	2	5	1	7	1	3	1	6	2
3	2	7	9	8	5	4	7	4	3	9	6	6	7	4	3
4	2	1	5	2	3	6	5	2	9	8	7	4	6	3	8
8	9	4	2	5	8	1	3	7	6	1	4	5	3	2	5
3	7	3	6	1	6	3	2	6	3	4	6	2	1	7	6
2	2	8	9	7	5	8	6	2	4	2	9	7	5	1	9
8	4	5	6	9	7	5	4	5	6	5	6	8	5	1	0

"Simulate a perilous path through the puzzle, Watson. Starting at the '1' in the top left-hand corner and ending at the '0' in the bottom right-hand corner, trace one path that consists of number segments. You can only move horizontally or vertically, and each number in each segment must be different. When you encounter a number already used, you must turn left or right and continue onto a new segment."

Look for the thatched roofs of a hamlet on the map.

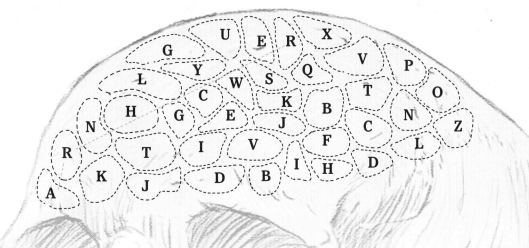

"I confess; I covet your cranium, Mr. Holmes!" Dr. Mortimer admits. "Cranial analysis of great men's skulls is a passion in which I indulge without restraint."

"Thank you. I feel flattered," responds Holmes. "I know and respect Franz Joseph Gall's work on phrenology. He was searching for clues about the mind's functions using the bumps on a person's head. Indeed, in my line of work, nothing is more precious than the observation of unexpected bumps on an otherwise level surface to find a clue leading to a solution.

"Look, Watson, there is a logical way to move across this skull. To navigate from points A to Z, alternately use letters that are adjacent then the same."

> Count the bumps used in the path
> and go to that number on the map.

"Etched into Fox Tor, one of Dartmoor's renowned rock formations, are enough letters to spell TOR in many ways by following the adjacent letters both horizontally and vertically".

The number of ways that spell "TOR" will tell you where to go next on the map.

Facing Horror

"As you know, Watson, facial expressions are closely linked to a person's feelings. Even though many people are taught from early on to suppress and hide any visible trace of their emotions, horror is such an overpowering, uncontrollable feeling that it can obliterate such training and distort a person's face.

"Here, Sir Henry Baskerville's face is disfigured by the sight of that horrific beast in several ways."

Count the number of different types of faces made by Sir Henry, add 4, and go there on the map.

A Foolscap Jigsaw

"A wastebasket can be a trove of clues, Watson. Here are the first cutouts made by Mrs. Stapleton before she produced the message she pasted onto foolscap paper and sent it to Sir Henry. She composed a sentence that differed by only one word from the sentence she ultimately sent, which reads, 'As you value your life or your reason, keep away from the moor.'

"What word was changed?"

Count the letters of the word
that was not included in the sent
message, add 10, and go there
on the map.

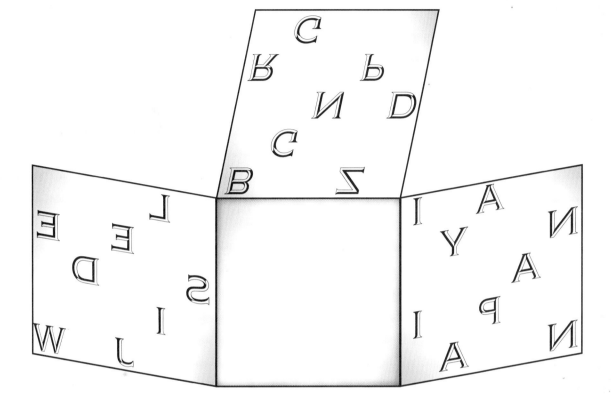

"The heroic beast became so famous when it killed Sir Henry's ancestor Sir Hugo Baskerville that its description was etched into a piece of jewelry. To read it, fold the three squares of glass over the center square.

"Can you decipher what it says, Wotson?"

> The number of words, plus 2, tells you where you should go next on the map.

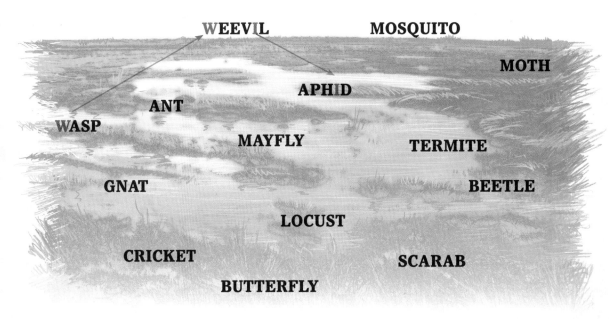

"Mr. Jack Stapleton's choice of entomology as a hobby is excellent on this moor, where insects thrive," Holmes contemplates. "It gives him an excuse to roam the land anywhere at anytime.

"How can we join these fourteen insects so that each name has exactly one letter in common with the next?"

> Go to a high place on the moor
> on the map.

A Blazing Hound

"This vessel contains an essential part of our mystery," Holmes explains. "The chemical is immersed in water because it is highly flammable when exposed to air and oxygen. Mr. Stapleton rubbed some of it onto his huge hound, transforming the dog into a supernatural monster.

"Your knowledge of chemistry should have tipped you off, Watson. The creature that assaulted us smelled like garlic, a characteristic of this chemical when it's burning. What chemical?"

Go to an advertisement promoting
perfumes on the map.

Boots and Knots

"Look at Sir Henry's boots, Watson. After the loss of one boot yesterday, the valet who attends to the boots at the Northumberland Hotel made sure this would not happen again. He knotted the laces tightly together."

Count the number of knots made when you pull the laces and head there on the map.

The Prison Lock

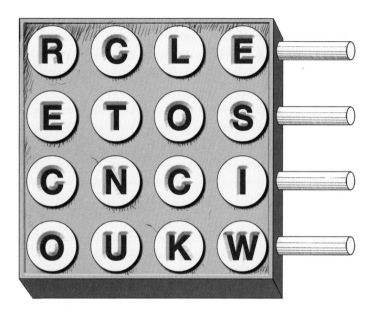

"Interesting," murmurs Holmes while inspecting the prison's new lock system. "They replaced all the conventional locks with this new technology. A guard doesn't need a set of keys anymore. Each door has a clever system of pins and wheels that controls the opening of the lock—if you press the keys in the right order—which explains how a smart convict could escape. He was sharp enough to detect and punch the keyword.

"What sixteen-letter word do the keys spell that must be punched in a continuous line on the keypad?"

Find a traditional type of
puzzle on the map
and go there.

Framing Masters

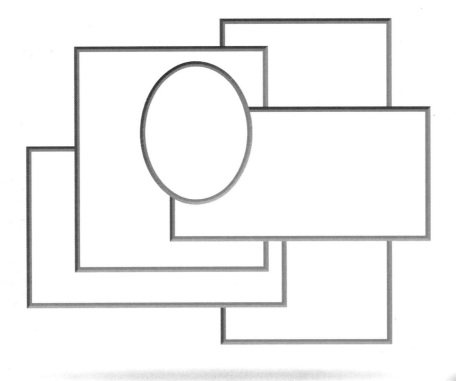

"**A**lthough I'm glad we passed through this art gallery and could compare the talents of the Belgian masters," Holmes notes, "forget the art, Watson, and notice that the paintings' frames offer an interesting geometric problem.

"Suppose they were pulled together and made transparent so that we could only see their borders. How many nonoverlapping areas would the frames define?"

Go and wait for Inspector
Lestrade at the train station
on the map.

"Blacksmiths usually do not forge numbers into wrought iron, yet Baskerville Hall's gate is adorned with them.

"Can you find the craftsman's intentional logical flaw in them?" Holmes asks. "It seems he expected only a brilliant mind like mine to notice."

Add together the digits of the
wrong number and go there
on the map.

Key Clues

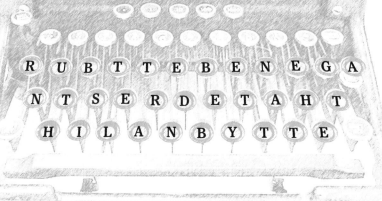

R U B T T E B E N E G A
N T S E R D E T A H T
H I L A N B Y T T E

"See how smart Miss Stapleton was!" Holmes admires. "Even though she obeyed her husband, Jack, and typed the message that would send Sir Charles Baskerville to his death, she still managed to leave traces of the words she typed on the typewriter's keys.

"The message can be read by following the letters on adjacent keys, both horizontally and diagonally."

Find a glowing dog on the map.

  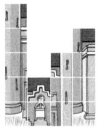  

"With its two high towers, Baskerville Hall is a formidable sight. I can easily see why the shameful legacy of its infamous seventeenth-century crime is etched into the architecture.

"A keyword about the case is hidden in the building's façade, in which some squares spell out the cause of the crime. Although a couple of squares recently fell, can you figure out the fateful word if you were to imagine them back in place?" Holmes asks Watson.

> Find the wooden gate where Sir Henry Baskerville met the beast on the map.

A Whiff of a Clue

A	B	J	V	E	T	I	V	E	J	E	A
G	B	E	R	G	A	M	O	T	E	H	C
A	M	S	U	V	E	B	E	W	S	I	E
R	Y	S	A	N	D	A	L	W	S	O	D
G	R	A	F	R	O	S	E	N	A	E	A
A	R	M	O	N	X	I	M	C	M	L	R
L	H	I	L	K	A	L	I	A	I	K	O
B	E	N	A	X	L	P	O	R	N	I	S
A	J	E	S	S	A	M	I	N	E	L	E
N	A	L	P	R	E	D	N	E	V	A	L
U	P	X	I	L	U	O	H	C	T	A	P
M	L	K	N	E	X	K	S	I	R	R	O
L	A	V	E	N	D	E	R	K	X	A	L

AGAR

BASIL

BERGAMOT

CARDAMON

CEDAR

ELEMI

GALBANUM

JESSAMINE

LAVENDER

MYRRH

ORRIS

PATCHOULI

PINE

ROSE

SANDALWOOD

VETIVER

"Here again, Watson, my highly trained sense of smell alerted me that the message on the foolscap paper was composed by a woman," Holmes declares. "Therefore, well before we headed to Devon, I was prepared to meet a lady playing an active role in the adventure who was wearing a specific perfume fragrance, which is among the seventy-five I'm able to identify. Which scent is included three times and worn by Mrs. Stapleton?"

Go to the next page.

Chapter Clue

"Did you notice a tiny but strange mistake in this chapter, Watson? Ah, of course, you couldn't see it because your mind is not trained to notice the small discrepancies that I, as a detective, call clues. These details, generally unheeded by ordinary mortals, are the essential stones on which I build my solutions to the mysteries."

The anomaly you found in this chapter is a clue to the final word puzzle. Make a note of the letter and save it below to solve the puzzle on page 163, after you have gone through the six adventures in the book.

Clue for chapter 4: _____

CHAPTER 5

The Red-Headed League

This adventure opposes Holmes's logic to the extreme, and one wonders why the great detective was called in at all! There is no crime, except for a patent discrepancy in the well-ordered Victorian world. Mr. Jabez Wilson, the client, is a well-travelled red-headed chap who has explored as far as China and likes to show it off by flaunting his jewels and tattoos. He is now a shopkeeper in London and is deeply disturbed by the obvious lack of logic in his current situation. He was offered a job, and was well paid for it by an organization that suddenly disappeared.

Instead of accepting his good fortunes, particularly as the organization left no debt, the red-headed client seeks out Detective Holmes, who is immediately fascinated by the case. He agrees with his client that such an absurd situation cannot be allowed to remain unexplained.

As explained in the introduction, tear out the map attached to this chapter and keep it with you as a travel guide. It will be essential for steering you through the strange places and events within this chapter.

Start with the first puzzle on the next page, solve it, and then follow the boxed hint to find the next puzzle number on the map. With the puzzle's number above the title, go to the corresponding puzzle in the chapter.

Repeat this sequence with each puzzle, going back and forth from the puzzles to the map and back again, until you reach the last case.

A Study in Red

"Our client's hair is remarkable, Watson. As a red-head, he displays more than one fiery color. He is a true study in red.

"At first glance, I see as many as ten different shades, yet one shade on the list is not among the shades of red above."

RED
CHERRY
ROSE
JAM
RUBY
WINE
BRICK
BLOOD
BERRY
CANDY
BLUSH

The rank of the missing shade in
the list indicates where to go next
on the map.

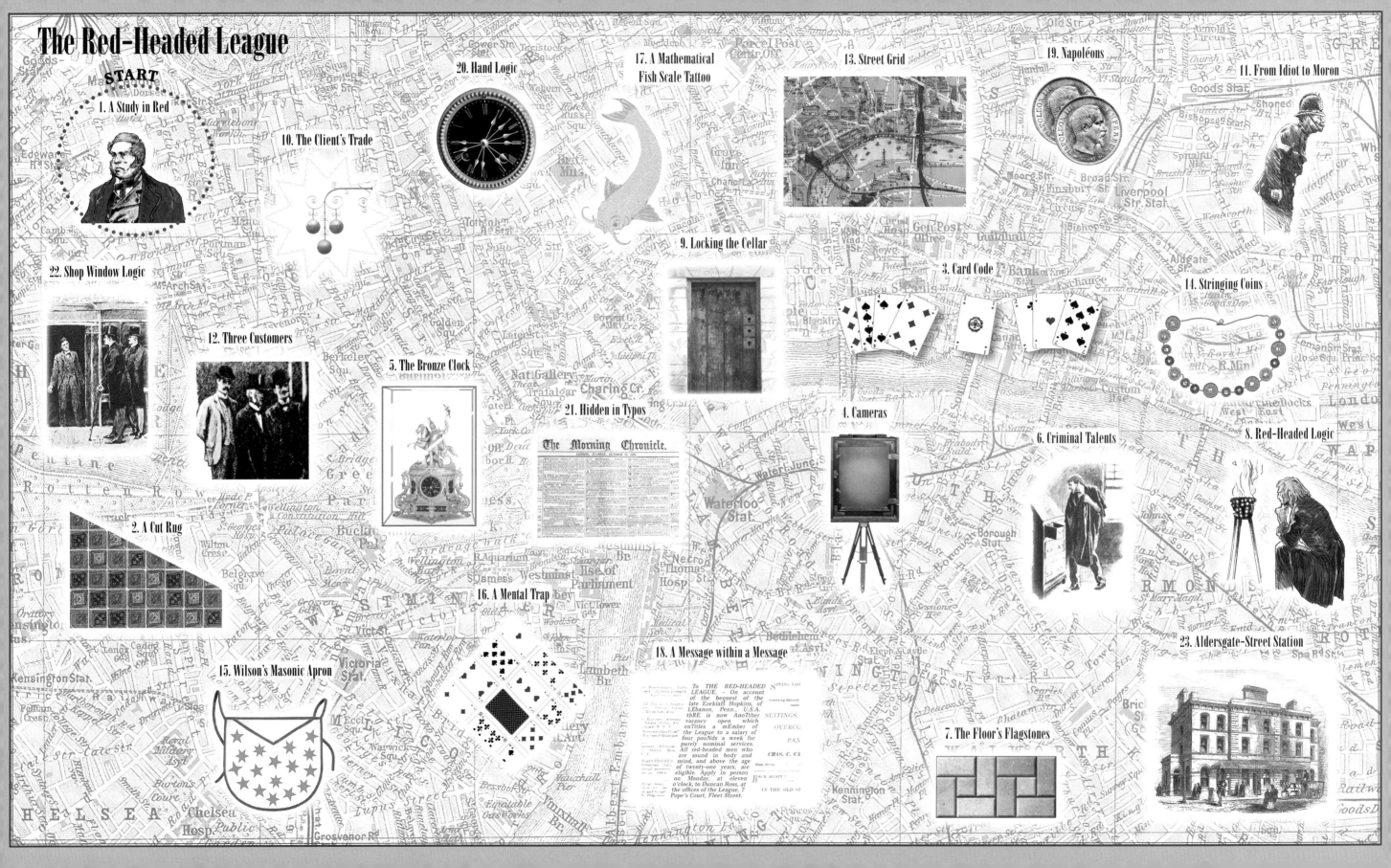

The Red-Headed League

START

1. A Study in Red

20. Hand Logic

17. A Mathematical Fish Scale Tattoo

13. Street Grid

19. Napoléons

11. From Idiot to Moron

10. The Client's Trade

22. Shop Window Logic

9. Locking the Cellar

3. Card Code

14. Stringing Coins

12. Three Customers

5. The Bronze Clock

21. Hidden in Typos

4. Cameras

6. Criminal Talents

8. Red-Headed Logic

2. A Cut Rug

16. A Mental Trap

23. Aldersgate-Street Station

15. Wilson's Masonic Apron

18. A Message within a Message

7. The Floor's Flagstones

CHAPTER 5

The Red-Headed League

MAP

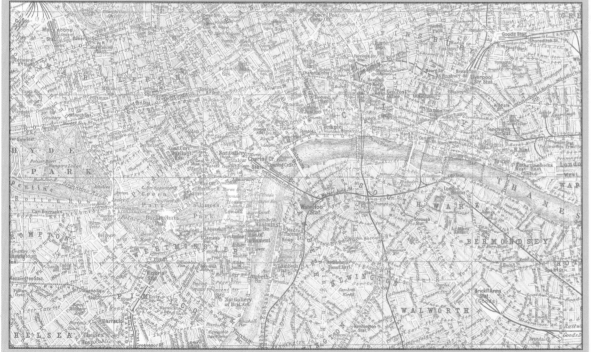

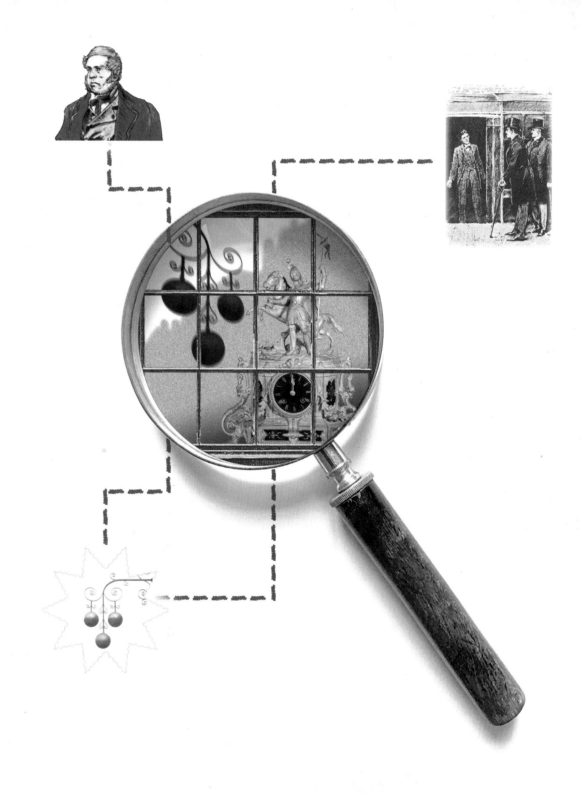

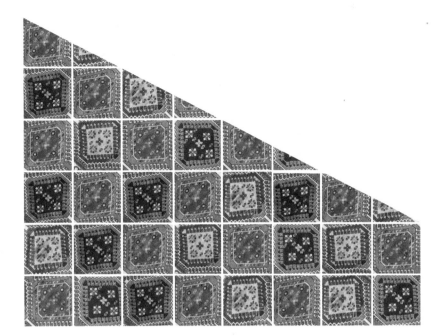

"I see a section of a beautiful antique Persian rug in the window, Watson, but at such a low price the shopkeeper must not know its true value. Let's get it and see how far we can impose our own logic."

"We are interested in this inexpensive piece of rug, Mr. Wilson. I wonder if you would be willing to sell it to John Watson and me, in such a way that we would both get exactly half of the area? We'd insist that it be cut in one straight line, of course, so the overall pattern is altered as little as possible."

"I'm afraid I wouldn't be able to do exactly that, Mr. Holmes, although I'll do my best to oblige."

"You are mistaken, Sir. The cutting we require can be done easily enough."

After you determine where to divide the rug into two, count the number of uncut squares in each piece and head there on the map.

"   brought a pack of cards, but I see the criminals have a taste for cards,
too," Holmes notices. "They left part of an ongoing game on top of a crate.
No, on second thought, these cards must have been left here on purpose. They are
obviously a message for expected accomplices.

"Can you read the message, Watson?"

The number of letters of the
message tells you where to
go on the map.

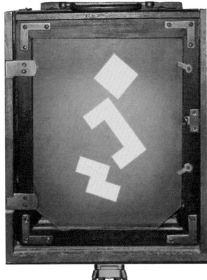

"To help him prepare for his crime, our thief took pictures of the shop's cellar with two cameras, which are equipped with two different lenses to deliver two different magnifications," Holmes explains. "The right hand one doubles the size of the pictures. We tested them on a square of cardboard that was cut into five pieces, adding a sixth piece that doesn't belong.

"Which cardboard piece doesn't belong to the square?"

Count the basic squares of the pieces that belong, add 3, and go there on the map.

The Bronze Clock

"Since we suspect the villain handled this bronze clock, its glass showcase is of the upmost importance. Our thief's fingerprints are very likely on it. Some fingers left several prints; let's see how many different fingers actually touched the glass?" Holmes suggests.

Find the close-up of the clockface on the map.

Criminal Talents

```
S  M  A  S  H  E  R  T  H  I  E  F  F  O  R  G  E  R
M  U  R  D  E  R  E  R  F  R  A  U  D  F  E  L  O  N
V  I  L  L  A  I  N  O  F  F  E  N  C  E  D  E  R  S
C  R  O  O  K  T  R  A  I  T  O  R  H  U  S  T  L  E
R  A  C  K  E  T  E  E  R  E  S  W  I  N  D  L  E  R
H  O  U  S  E  B  R  E  A  K  I  N  G  A  R  S  O  N

A  V  E  R  E  E  T  E  K  C  A  R  E  L  T  S  U  H
D  U  A  R  F  R  E  L  D  N  I  W  S  N  O  S  R  A
E  F  H  R  E  H  S  A  M  S  R  E  R  E  D  R  U  M
N  O  L  E  F  L  O  K  O  O  R  C  R  O  T  A  R  T
U  R  E  G  R  O  F  S  E  C  N  E  F  O  R  Z  E  N
M  N  I  A  L  L  I  V  L  E  D  N  F  E  I  H  T  A
```

"I must give our thieves some credit, Watson. Our hidden adversaries are remarkably inventive. A criminal career offers almost more opportunities than an honest one! Consider the quantity of words about their evil trade in the dictionary. A quick survey brings no less than fifteen terms for crimes and their perpetrators.

"Which word is only found in the upper part of the grid?"

The number of letters of the word tells you where to go on the map.

The Floor's Flagstones

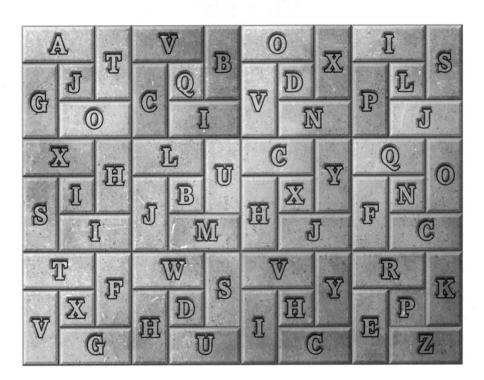

"While we wait for the villains to push up a flagstone from below and appear in this cellar, there is no harm in exercising our minds, Watson! I suggest you imagine there is a letter on each flagstone and attempt to go from the top-left A to the bottom-right Z through a bizarre maze.

"Connect A to Z by jumping alternately to a letter on an adjacent flagstone with a contiguous side, and then to a remote stone having an identical letter."

Head for a railway station
on the map.

Red-Headed Logic

NOBODY WHO LOVES POETRY HATES MUSIC.

RED-HEADS ARE WITLESS WHEN ADAMANT.

ONE CAN'T BE TRULY CREATIVE WITHOUT SOME DAYDREAMING.

CREATIVITY IS CHARACTERISTIC OF GENIUS.

DAYDREAMERS LOVE POETRY.

WITLESS PEOPLE HATE MUSIC IF THEY HAVE LONG HAIR.

"Watson, if you accept these six assumptions above and apply logic, do you think an adamant red-head can be a genius if he has long hair?"

Go to a display on the map devised to trap a genius.

Locking the Cellar

"The cellar is the place where the crime is expected to take place. Did you try to lock it before you left for work?" Holmes asks the shopkeeper.

"No, I didn't. Three people need access to the cellar: my salesperson, housekeeper, and the superintendent, he replies"

"You are mistaken, Sir. There is a way to install three locks and distribute the keys to the people concerned so that none of them can open all the locks alone, yet can nonetheless gain access if another one of them is there, too."

Holmes asks Watson: "How can they manage the locks on the cellar door and how many keys would they have to distribute?"

Multiply the number of necessary keys by **3** and head there on the map.

The Client's Trade

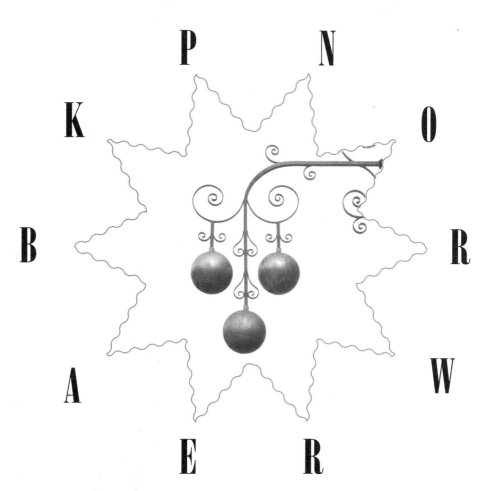

P   N

K   O

B   R

A   W

E   R

"I wonder how our client Mr. Wilson, after travelling as far as Asia, chose such an uneventful business?" Holmes thinks aloud.

Jump over a constant number of letters around the star, counterclockwise, to read the trade of Holmes's client.

> Go to the map and find
> the client's shop.

From Idiot to Moron

CHUMP   FOOL

CRETIN   DUNCE

PRAT   TWIT

IDIOT

CLOD   BERK

NINNY

HALFWIT   GOOF

BOZO

DUMMY   CLOT

STUPID

MORON

"I'm happy Inspector Peter Jones is helping us tonight," Holmes confides to Watson. "Although an absolute imbecile in his profession, he has one positive virtue. He is as brave as a bulldog and as tenacious as a lobster. Some might describe Jones with a term milder than 'imbecile.'

"Note that these eighteen synonyms can be arranged in a series, from IDIOT to MORON, where no two contiguous words have a common letter. For example IDIOT can link to CHUMP or to JERK. Can you do it?"

> The number of letters
> of the longest synonym
> tells you where to go
> next on the map.

Three Customers

"Our client's shop is the right place to test the logic of such a business. Watson, let's quiz these three friends coming out with gifts they just purchased. What can you say about your purchases, Sirs?"

"Had I bought silver, I'd have spent the least," Alex replies.

"The ruby was the most expensive," Caleb responds.

"I spent more than Caleb and more than the one who bought gold," Bert answers.

"Thank you, Gentlemen, this is enough to know who bought what. Enough for you too, Watson?"

> Count the number of letters of the gold
> buyer's first name, add 1, and head there
> on the map.

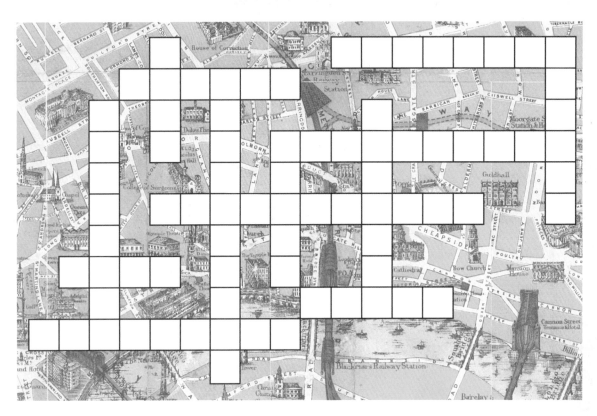

"*O*ur great city is a complex arrangement of streets that an accomplished detective needs to master in order to successfully outwit criminals.

"As a useful training, Watson, I suggest you complete this crossword with thirteen of the streets we saw while walking to Saxe-Coburg Square."

The number of letters of the street name crossing BAKER on K indicates your next step on the map.

BAKER
THAYER
MONDEVILLE
MARGARET
WELLS
NEWMAN
THEOBALDS
CLERKENWELL
BLOOMSBURY
BOND
SYCAMORE
GOSWELL
VERE

Stringing Coins

"Our client is very fond of China, Watson. Not only does he wear a Chinese coin on his watch chain, but he also has a necklace of Chinese coins. However, I must object to the arrangement of the coins on the necklace. It would have been perfectly logical except for one important detail.

"Do you see which coin is displaced and spoils the logic of the chain, Watson?"

The position of the first misplaced coin, counting from the top left, reveals where to head next on the map.

Wilson's Masonic Apron

"As a Freemason, our client has his own symbolic apron and wears it to the brotherhood's meetings.

"Analyzing the symbols displayed on the apron, I think it shows his birth year. Do you see why, Watson?"

> The last digit of the client's birth
> year tells you your next step
> on the map.

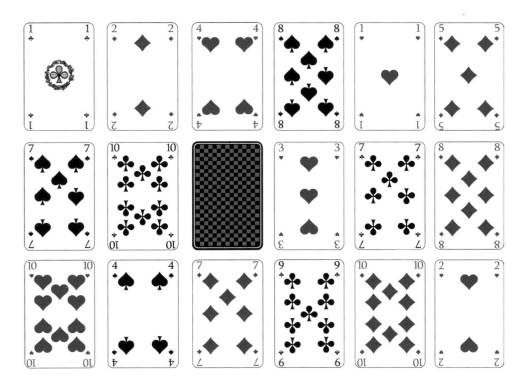

"I dare say, Watson, our adversary may be the fourth-smartest man in London, which provides us with an excellent opportunity to distract him with an intellectual card trap using my card deck. He will surely try to beat it. Ignoring all caution, he will irresistibly be tempted to turn over the main card to validate his pick. But, by handling the card, he will inadvertently leave his fingerprints on it and we'll put them to good use!

"What card is facedown?"

Count the pips of the facedown card, add 3, and go there on the map.

A Mathematical Fish Scale Tattoo

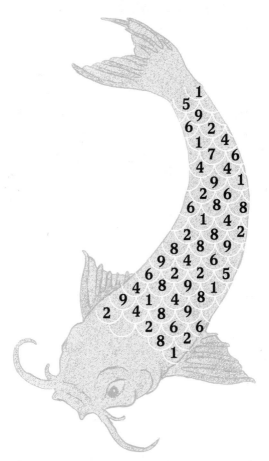

"Did you notice our client's Chinese carp tattoo, Watson? The fish scales evoke a digital grid, with numbers representing each scale. And like a 'scale,' the numbers in the grid are balanced. Each number is coupled with another number within a different scale that is its complement to 10, as in 1 and 9, or 4 and 6.

"Only one digit is left with no complement. Which is it?"

> Double the value of the lone
> digit to know where to go
> next on the map.

A Message within a Message

To THE RED-HEADED LEAGUE. - *On account of the bequest of the late EzekiaH Hopkins, of LEbanon, Penn., U.S.A. thRE is now AnoTther vacancy open which enTitles a mEmber of the League to a salary of four pouNds a week for purely nominal services. All red-headed men who are sound in body and mind, and above the age of twenty-one years, are eligible. Apply in person on Monday, at eleven o'clock, to Duncan Ross, at the offices of the League, 7 Pope's Court, Fleet Street.*

"How fascinating, Watson! Look at the advertisement in *The Morning Chronicle*. The author found a way of publishing a message within a message so that millions of readers would read it, but only one person would fully understand it. At first glance, you would think the typographer who set the text mistook lowercase letters for uppercase ones. However, this common error occurs so often that we have to assume it was done intentionally.

"What do you make of it, Watson?"

> Go to the newspaper
> on the map.

Napoléons

"The criminals cut up some coins not only to hide them better but also to melt them down before reselling them.

"How many complete, original Napoléons are on the table, Watson?"

When you find out the original number
of coins, head there on the map.

"I tell you, Watson, this clock is particularly challenging, and it must be the work of that extremely smart criminal we are chasing. Although, at first, it appears he gathered a bunch of minute hands and pinned them onto a dial, I am sure he didn't do it randomly. There is a logical method to the way they point to the minutes if we consider the minutes as a series.

"If he were to pin one more minute hand onto the dial, to follow the same logic, where would the hand point?"

> The minute value pointed at by the new hand,
> divided by 6, indicates where to go on the map.

Hidden in Typos

To THE RED-HEADED LEAGUE. - On account of thE beQuest of thE late Ezekiah Hopkins, oF Lebanon, Penn., U.S.A. thrE is Now Another vacancy open Which entitLes a membEr of tHe League to a salary Of Four pOunds a week fOr purely nominal services. All red-headed men who are sound in body and mind, and above the age of Twenty-one years, are eligible. Apply in person on Monday, at eLeVen o'cloCk, to Duncan ROss, at the offices of the League, 7 Pope's Court, Fleet Street.

"This hidden message trick goes further than you think, Watson. I sent for the evening edition of *The Morning Chronicle* and was rewarded. 'The Red-Heads' advertisement is there again, but with different typos! Like before, some letters are in uppercase for no obvious reason, but reading them, as we did this morning, yields no message. The key is certainly different, even if similar to the previous one. What is it?

"Can you read the new message?"

> Add 13 to the number of
> words in the message to know
> where to go next on the map.

Shop Window Logic

RUG
2

LOCKET
8

NECKLACE
15

ORMOLU
?

PAPERWEIGHT
28

THIMBLE
10

BULLION
12

DIAMOND
12

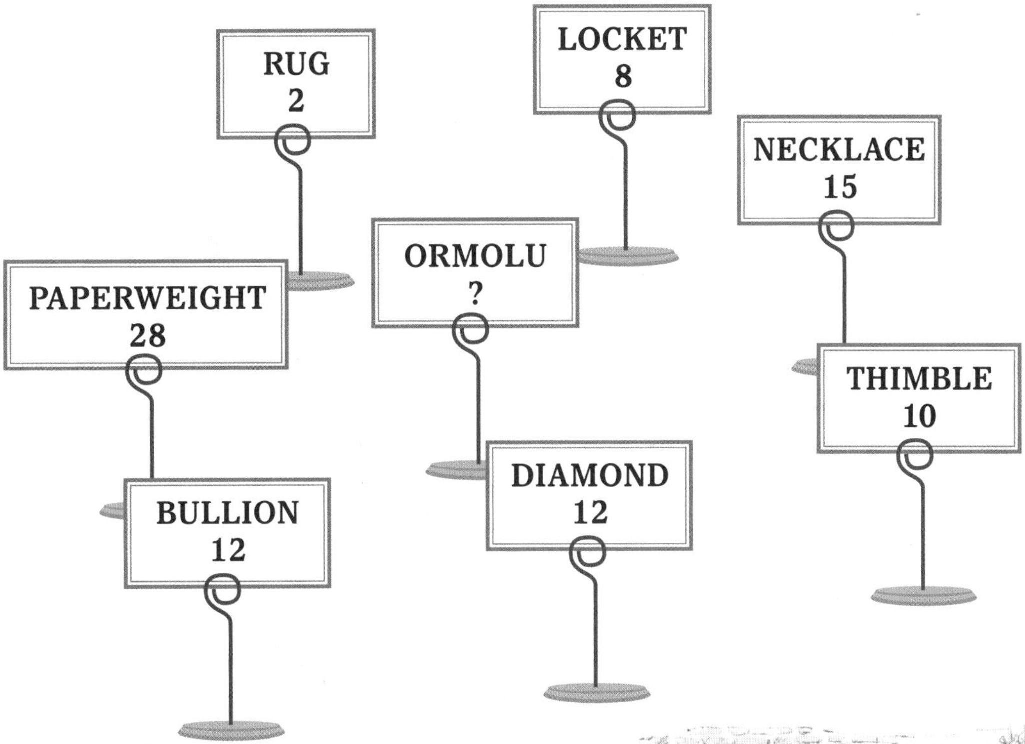

"As can be expected in his trade, Watson, our client's shop window displays a wide variety of goods. However, there is an obvious price-setting method, which makes it easy to guess the missing price for the *ormolu*, which is how professionals refer to gilded-bronze objects."

Go to the least expensive item in the shop on the map.

Aldersgate-Street Station

"Aldersgate-Street windows must have been highly impressed by the villain's craftiness since they advertise it. They devised a way of describing his activity without spelling it out directly.

"Can you grasp the system and read the message, Watson?"

Proceed to the next page.

Chapter Clue

"Did you notice a tiny but strange mistake in this chapter, Watson? Ah, of course, you couldn't see it because your mind is not trained to notice the small discrepancies that I, as a detective, call clues. These details, generally unheeded by ordinary mortals, are the essential stones on which I build my solutions to the mysteries."

The anomaly you found in this chapter is a clue to the final word puzzle. Make a note of the letter and save it below to solve the puzzle on page 163, after you have gone through the six adventures in the book.

Clue for chapter 5: _____

CHAPTER 6

The Adventure of the Naval Treaty

This adventure begins in London's Foreign Office, a core command center during the Victorian era when England controlled a major part of the world. Throughout this story, our modern eyes are surprised that such an important government organization seemed to be so little concerned with its security.

During the evenings, the Foreign Office is guarded by one sleepy commissionaire, whose most formidable weapon is a kettle. In addition, nobody seems to bat an eyelid when he occasionally dozes off or receives a visit from his wife. More astounding, still, is that when a sensitive document is stolen, the officer, Mr. Perry Phelps, is held responsible while the commissionaire isn't even deemed a suspect.

Sherlock Holmes's talents are immediately required, for only logic and a superior intellect can possibly resolve such a breach of security. Our famous detective widens his search and, without fail, finds the document in a most unexpected place!

As explained in the introduction, tear out the map attached to this chapter and keep it with you as a travel guide. It will be essential for steering you through the strange places and events within this chapter.

Start with the first puzzle on the next page, solve it, and then follow the boxed hint to find the next puzzle number on the map. With the puzzle's number above the title, go to the corresponding puzzle in the chapter.

Repeat this sequence with each puzzle, going back and forth from the puzzles to the map and back again, until you reach the last case.

Litmus Test

"Why, hello, Watson. I'm dipping a piece of litmus paper into this vessel to see what kind of result I obtain, as a man's life depends on the reading.

"What does the smoke spell?"

Head on the map to another type of vessel that uses a technology powered by nature.

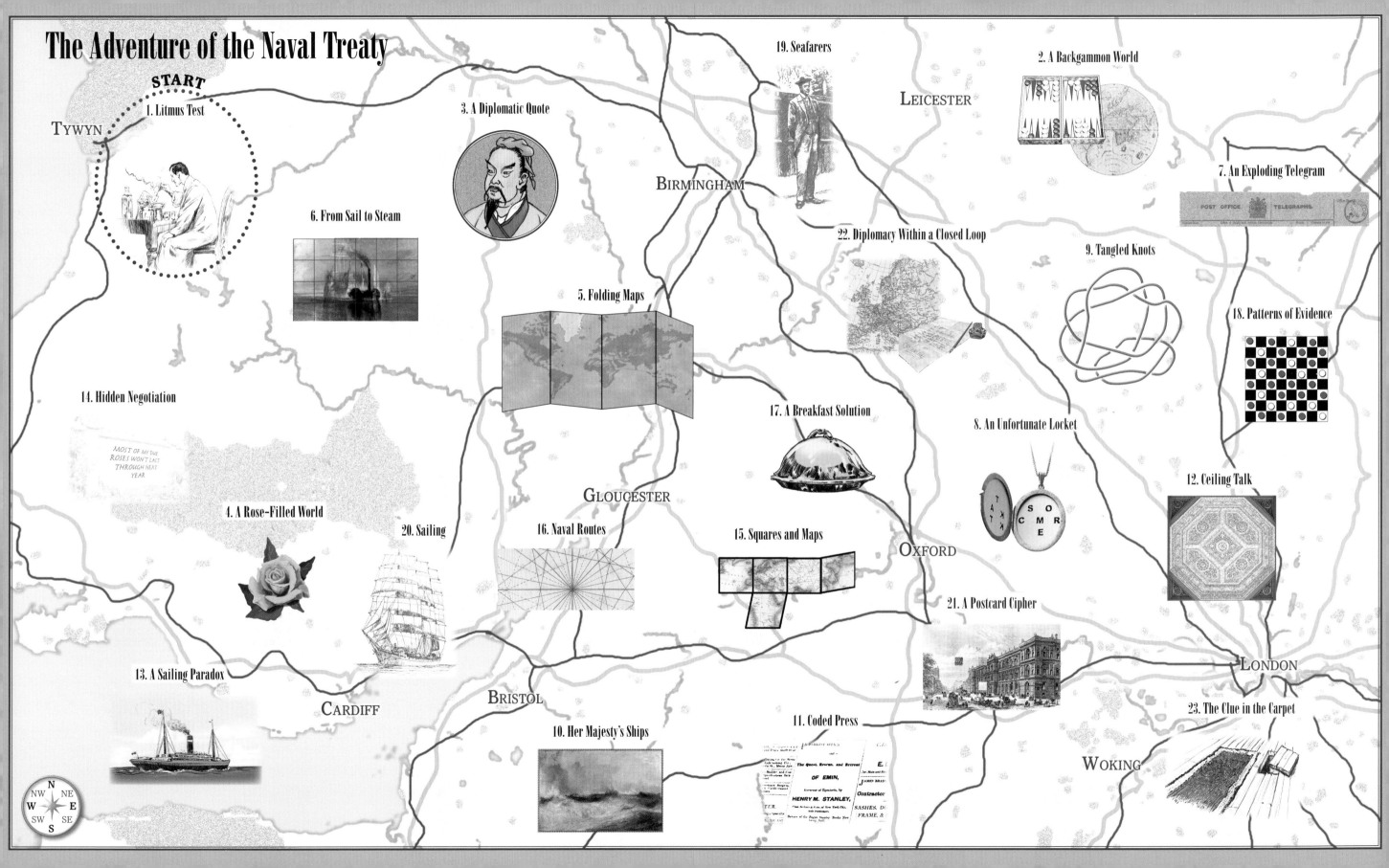

⚜ CHAPTER 6 ⚜

The Adventure of the Naval Treaty

MAP

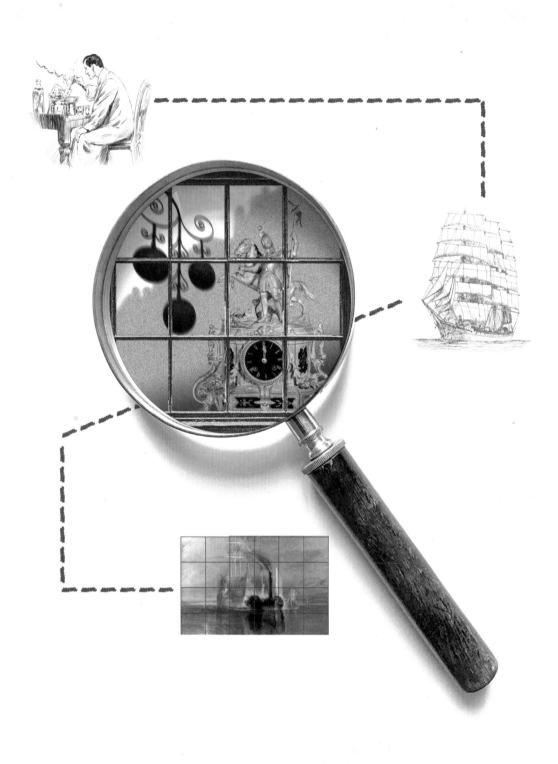

A Backgammon World

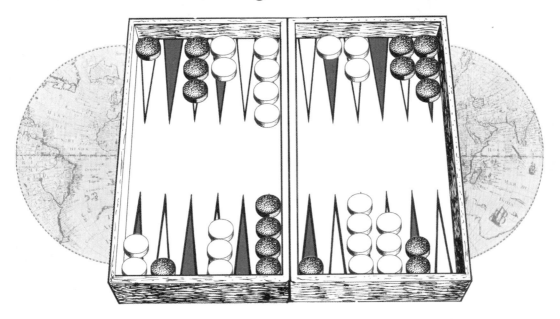

"The backgammon board is a good example of the naval world and why they need to have sound treaties, Watson. Like checkers traveling from point to point around the board's four quadrants, ships sail through the oceans hoping to reach their destination, often close to enemy ships. Just as backgammon players need rules, ships require solid, coherent pacts to ensure that a peaceful climate makes business possible. If there is a logical flaw in an agreement, war is then inescapable.

"Do you see the logical flaw within the quadrants of this backgammon layout?"

Find a wall bearing a hidden
message on the map.

A Diplomatic Quote

E	H	E	A	E	G	E	N	E	M	E		A	I	B	D	O
F	T	T	F	I	U	H	R	E	T	G		S	R	T	H	O
T		W	H	R		I	S	I	M	O		W	U	T		U
U			S		P	T		N	Y							

T	H	E														O
								G								

"We must proceed with the utmost care, Watson, for we are in the dubious world, where lowly crime imperils high diplomacy. It's time to unearth a quote from the great Chinese military strategist Sun Tzu.

"Can you read his precept by dropping each letter from the upper grid into its correct square below, in the same column of the lower grid, Watson? Each letter may only be used once."

Go to a more geometrical treatment of diplomacy seen as a loop on the map.

A Rose-Filled World

CHUCKLES DUCHER MOZART
NAPOLEON SITKA VANITY
ALBA ADAM DORTMUND
ALOHA BOLERO ERFURT PINKIE
SPICE TWIST

"I admire roses, Watson, and I have the greatest admiration for botanists and growers who cultivate new varieties in their nurseries, sometimes naming their creations after celebrities.

"Proceeding from Napoleon to Mozart, can you link the different varieties that have no common letters?"

On the map, go to explore the logic of representing the world with squares.

5
Folding Maps

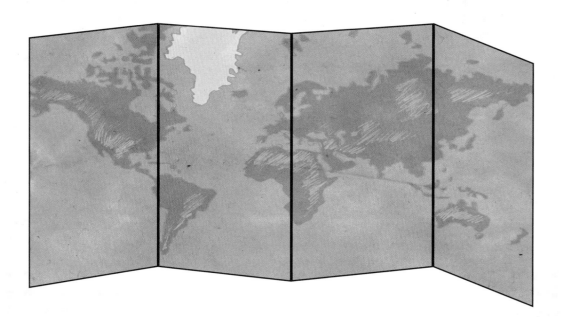

"Another problem with maps, Watson, is that they need to be folded, which can often be done in several ways. The standard method for folting a four-part map, such as this one, yields a surprising number of solutions. "How many ways can you fold the four sections of the map into a single one?"

Count the number of solutions and
head there on the map.

From Sail to Steam

"Watson, I must admit that, disregarding the pointless emotions one may feel in front of J.M.W. Turner's painting *The Fighting Temeraire Tugged to Her Last Berth to Be Broken Up*, I'm personally intrigued by the symbol he painted on the canvas. A small steamboat is tugging a huge, majestic sailing ship to its last mooring, demonstrating the power of steam over wind and the beginning of our modern era.

"Fortunately, logic plays a role here. The picture is copied on top of a checkerboard that is missing some squares. Can you cut it into two exact halves along the lattice lines?"

Go to a necklace with a message on the map.

An Exploding Telegram

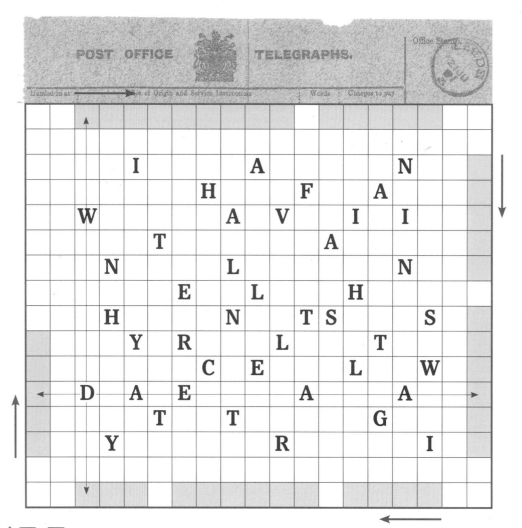

POST OFFICE   TELEGRAPHS.

Office Stamp.

Handed in at ⟶ ...ce of Origin and Service Instructions   Words   Charges to pay

"How explosive, Watson, if that telegram were revealed and published in the papers! For the time being, however, it's hidden within this exploding grid. The words' letters are in the center, ready to burst outward into the purple squares to read clockwise.

"Can you slide each letter back in place, either horizontally or vertically, while remaining within the same row or column?"

Move on to an
evening paper
on the map.

"Joseph Harrison wears a locket as a reminder of his guilt and misfortunes. It bears the name of the place where he lost more money than he could afford, which could possibly turn him into a criminal. Notice how the secret is especially well protected, for it can never be spelled out clearly.

"Can you visualize what is says when the locket is closed, Watson?"

> Find a
> pleasantly scented
> item on the map.

Tangled Knots

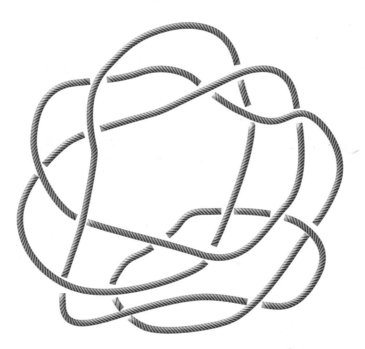

"Sail or steam, the navy would not be able to exist without ropes and knots, for they are the technology necessary for tugging, stowing, and fastening. Similarly, the logic of knots is often useful to understand entangled criminal cases, in addition to being an excellent way of training your logical thinking, Watson.

"If you were to pull this rope, how many knots would there be?"

> Head to the
> number of knots
> on the map.

Her Majesty's Ships

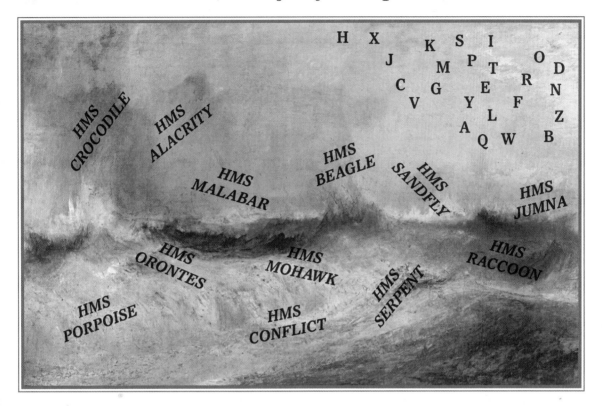

"I dare say, Watson, I should really apply my talents to language sometime. Words—their use and letters—defy ordinary logic and need to be studied in depth by a competent mind. Look at the most impressive ambassadors of our Majesty's power, Her Royal Navy, cruising around the world's oceans. All sorts of names are used to baptize Her Majesty's ships.

"However, only one of the names of the valorous ships in white cannot be spelled using the floating black letters inside the sea spray from J.M.W. Turner's painting *Waves Breaking against the Wind.*"

Go to the safer territory of a
breakfast table on the map.

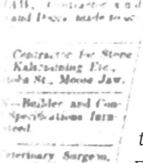

A£10 Revard. - The number of the cob whach dropped a fare al or about the door of the Poreign Effice in Charles Stleet, ot a quarten to ten an the everint of May 23rd. Apply 221B Baker Street

"I didn't receive any replies to the advertisement I published in the evening papers, Watson, but I am not surprised. I didn't expect any! My real motive was to send a hidden message to a colleague I have in the Foreign Office. If needed, he was ready to go and search Percy Phelps' office, but was waiting for a signal from me to ensure that Percy was away. Fortunately, I have a friend at one of the newspapers who was willing to risk his reputation as a typographer to set the text above.

"Can you read the coded message?"

> Go to the puzzle to the immediate northeast of this one on the map.

Ceiling Talk

"Do not let this ceiling surprise you, Watson. No place is more immersed in ciphers and secret messages than Whitehall. They keep inventing new methods to conceal their exchanges with their embassies and foreign contacts. Looking at the letters on this ceiling, I'm certain their arrangement is intended to assist us in our quest.

"Some letters stand out and spell a word. Can you figure out the logic behind their placement?"

> The letters that stand out
> spell where to head next on
> the map.

A Sailing Paradox

"Here is an interesting paradox, Watson, that demonstrates technology's limits. A merchant reaches his destination on a sailboat at a speed of six knots. In a hurry to return to his departure point, he disembarks from the sailboat and then boards a steamboat. He asks the captain to steam ahead so that the average overall speed of the round trip equals twelve knots.

"Can the steamboat captain accept this challenge, and, if so, what must be his speed?"

> Go and apply your logic to a
> checkerboard on the map.

Hidden Negotiation

> MOST OF MY DUE
> ROSES WON'T LAST
> THROUGH NEXT
> YEAR

"Aha! I knew it, Watson! The villain has already started negotiating the sale of his loot. Look at this message scribbled on the garden wall. It looks like childish nonsense, but if you figure out the code, the amount is clear enough.

"I'll give you a hint, Watson. Romans were fond of graffiti."

> **Find the scene of an exploding telegram on the map.**

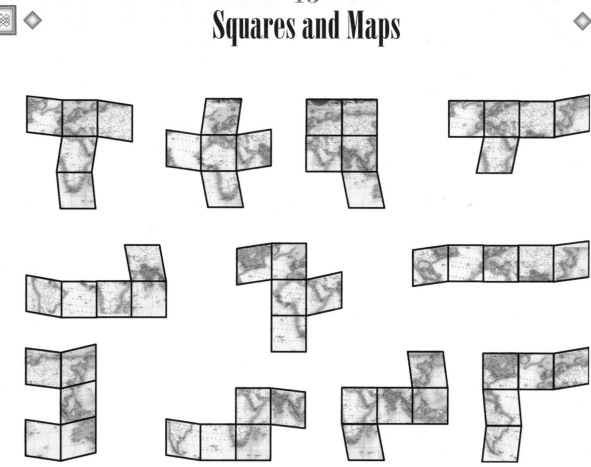

"Because it deals with the entire world, Watson, the Foreign Office contains a vast repository of maps. Their shapes vary according to the areas in question. Many of the maps can be displayed on a five-square surface. Yet, five squares can be assembled in twelve different ways, regardless of rotations or symmetries.

"Can you determine the twelfth possibility based on the eleven above?"

Go to the best method of
storing maps.

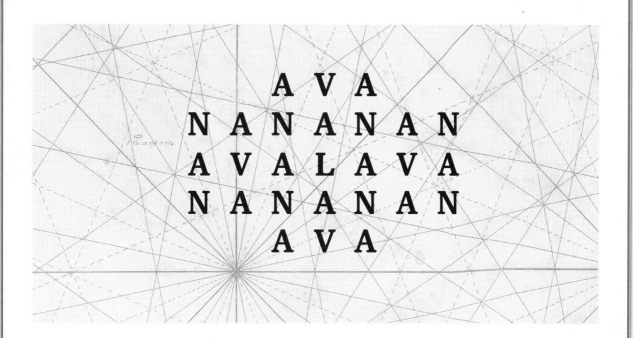

"There are many naval routes to get from one port to another when at sea, depending on how one makes use of the winds, currents, and time.

"Using the letters above, Watson, how many ways can you connect an N to the center L to spell out NAVAL using the adjacent letters but not the same letter twice in a word?"

Head to a black-and-red board
game on the map.

A Breakfast Solution

"Mr. Phelps, I can never resist a touch of the dramatic. I let your old friend Watson here prepare a surprise puzzle for you. The document you are looking for is under one of these plate covers. However, you must choose the correct cover.

"Using the table's logic, two numbers are out of order, and the plate cover that contains your missing document is in between the two."

A final clue awaits you inside
a carpet on the map.

Patterns of Evidence

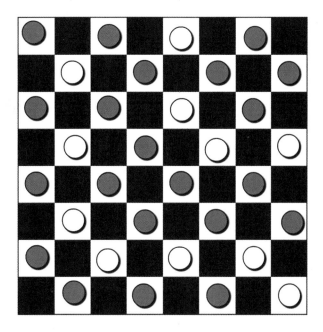

"The difficulty in your case," Holmes remarks to Phelps in his usual didactic fashion, "lay in the event of having too much evidence. Of all the facts that were presented to us, we had to pick only those that we deemed to be essential, and then piece them together to reconstruct this very remarkable chain of events. Interestingly, you have a similar situation on this checkerboard, where, like facts in a case, I have arranged black and white checkers based on a very simple pattern. However, one square does not follow the pattern, and thus holds a checker with the wrong color.

"Can you identify the patterns and reconstruct the correct order of squares?"

Go back to sea and look
for a painting of rough
weather on the map.

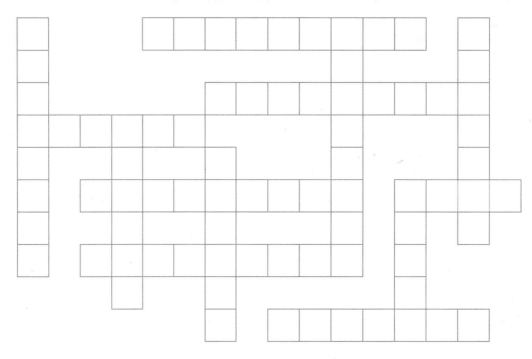

" The seafarer's trade is a very organized and hierarchical profession, Watson, with a number of positions you seldom see outside a vessel, including ARMOURER, BOATSWAIN, CARPENTER, CAULKER, CHAPLAIN, CLERK, COOK, MASTER, PURSER, ROPEMAKER, SAILMAKER, SEAMAN, SURGEON, and YEOMAN.

"One name cannot fit in the crossword. Can you guess it?"

> Explore a sailing
> paradox on the map.

Sailing

F	L	A	N	K	E	R
M	J	I	B	V	A	O
M	I	Z	Z	E	N	Y
Z	R	G	E	N	O	A
E	N	E	E	T	A	L
L	I	A	S	G	U	L
N	O	M	E	A	R	F

A	G	E	N	O	A	F
K	A	R	O	Y	A	L
Y	E	J	N	E	S	A
S	M	I	Z	Z	E	N
A	T	B	R	U	G	K
I	L	E	D	B	A	E
L	A	T	E	E	N	R

FLANKER
GENOA
GENNAKER
JIB
LATEEN
MAINSAIL
MIZZEN
RINGTAIL
ROYAL
SKYSAIL
SPINNAKER
SPRITSAIL
LUGSAIL
WINGSAIL
TURBOSAIL
ROTORSAIL

"I've been thinking, Watson. Although the delicate science of obtaining strong wind power in different weather conditions is becoming increasingly obsolete day by day, let's study it with this list of sails. Six of the sails are found in both squares.

"Can you find which sail is only in one square?"

Go to the transition from
sails to steam on the map.

"Here is some more evidence of the villain's criminal scheme, an altered postcard cipher of Whitehall that he was intending to send to an accomplice.

"The system is simple enough and is designed to indicate a precise time to his partner in crime. Do you see it?

"I'll give you a hint, Watson. Remember the message on the wall and look for a similar logic."

> When you know the exact time,
> go explore Whitehall's ceilings
> on the map.

Diplomacy within a Closed Loop

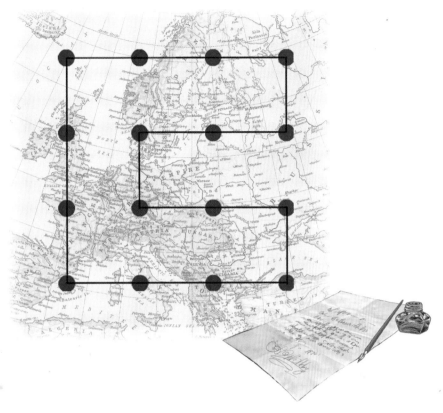

"Remember, Watson, that diplomacy is the art of aligning several nations in such a way so that each member serves the interest of all as much as possible. Let's say that these dots on the map represent sixteen countries, and that the seven lines represent a treaty or alliance. The lines go through each country exactly once and then close into a single group. However, there is a better way to group the countries so that the line remains closed, is comprised of six straight segments instead of seven, and goes through the sixteen countries exactly once.

"Can you draw that line, Watson?"

> Go to those men actually
> at sea on the map.

The Clue in the Carpet

"To conclude this adventure, Watson, let me point out that the final clue in recovering the original Naval Treaty that Percy Phelps lost was simply hidden within a figure inside a carpet.

"Start with the correct letter and then jump regularly over a constant number of vertices to spell the clue."

Go to the next page.

Chapter Clue

"Did you notice a tiny but strange mistake in this chapter, Watson? Ah, of course, you couldn't see it because your mind is not trained to notice the small discrepancies that I, as a detective, call clues. These details, generally unheeded by ordinary mortals, are the essential stones on which I build my solutions to the mysteries."

The anomaly you found in this chapter is a clue to the final word puzzle below.

Clue for chapter 6: _____

Final Word: _____

Now that you have gone through the six adventures of this book, you should have gathered the six clues to tackle the final word puzzle.

Piece the six clues together and guess the hidden entities that Sherlock Holmes never encounters because of his logical and practical mind, yet played an important role in the life of his literary father, Sir Arthur Conan Doyle.

(Answer on page 188.)

Answers to The Adventure of the Speckled Band

1. ☞ HELEN. *Go to #5 on map.*

2. ☞ 8 pieces are displaced in a loop. Here is the restored picture. *Go to #8 on map.*

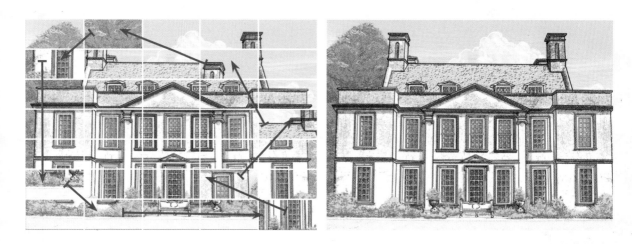

3. ☞ All numbers are multiples of 7, except 13. *Go to #13 on map.*

4. ☞ The ONCILLA is not in the rectangle. It is tenth in the list. *Go to #10 on map.*

```
D  N  R  E  G  I  T  H  C  T  A  C
N  O  I  L  E  U  R  C  G  U  O  C
R  A  U  Y  A  L  E  O  P  A  R  D
D  E  Z  N  O  Z  R  U  R  A  M  F
P  I  D  X  O  J  A  G  U  A  R  S
C  A  R  A  C  A  L  A  E  A  L  E
A  T  O  L  E  C  O  R  R  E  O  R
C  O  L  O  C  O  L  O  I  H  C  V
C  U  N  N  A  K  O  D  K  O  D  A
C  H  E  E  T  A  H  T  T  O  R  L
T  A  C  B  O  B  M  A  R  G  A  Y
```

5. ☞ 4 parts flipped over horizontally. 20 - 4 = 16. *Go to #16 on map.*

6. ☞ Synonyms of whistle: FLUTE, HISS, FIFE, SHRIEK, TOOT, WHIZ, TOOTLE, SKIRL, BLARE. The odd word is BAND, a key word of the present adventure. *Go to #17 on map.*

7. ☞ On every line but the second one, the hour is the product of the minute figures. *Go to #2 on map.*

8. ☞ BABOON, CAPUCHIN ,COLOBUS, DRILL, GEMLADA, LESULA, MACAQUE, MANDRILL, MARMOSET, PATAS, ROLOWAY, SAKI, TAMARIN, TITI, UAKARI, VERVET. Sherlock Holmes owned a Saki, which is fourth in the original list. *Go to #4 on map.*

9. ☞ Place the match to complete an E to read ADDER. *Go to #23 on map.*

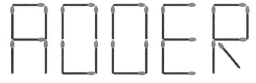

10. ☞ The central R reads RAN in 4 different ways. Each M reaches R in one way. This yields 4 x 4 = 16 MORANs. *Go to #6 on map.*

11. ☞ Pine tree means honeysuckle, which means no tiled roof, hence no brick wall, for they always go with a tiled roof. There is no pine tree in front of a tiled roof. *Go to #7 on map.*

◇ **Answers to The Adventure of the Speckled Band**

12. ☞ 11 straight lines.
Go to #22 on map.

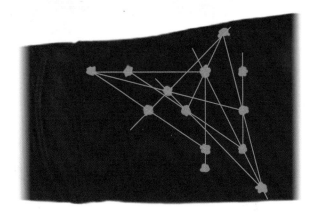

13. ☞ Barrel (B), Cylinder (Y), Frame (F), Screw (W), Guard (U) and Axis (X) : 6 + 5 = 11. *Go to #11 on map.*

14. ☞ There should be 3 three-pointed stars, 4 four-pointed stars, etc. One five-pointed star is missing on the band. *Go to #18 on map.*

15. ☞ If you pull the two ends of the leash, you get exactly one knot. *Go to #9 on map.*

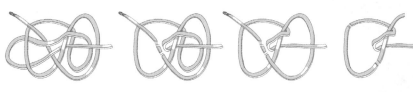

16. ☞ 4 triangles: 2 small ones and 2 bigger ones, each made of 2 parts. *Go to #19 on map.*

17. ☞ 3 pairs: AA, BB, and CC. *Go to #3 on map.*

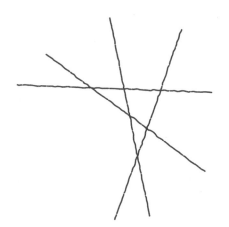

18. ☞ On each hexagon, opposite numbers add up to 10. Key number: 9. 9 + 11 = 20. *Go to #20 on map.*

19. ☞ PRACTITIONER (5-letter jumps). *Go to #12 on map.*

20. ☞ *Go to #21 on map.*

21. ☞ Price = 6/3. Numbers equal the letters of the two words. 6 + 9 = 15. *Go to #15 on map.*

22. ☞ On every string but the first one, there are two more red beads than green beads. *Go to #17 on map.*

23. ☞

M	A	M	B	A												
				N												
				A												
				C												
			■	C	O	B	R	A	■	U						
Y				O	N	D	A			R						
A				N	D					U						
R				D	A					T						A
A			■	A	S	P	■	U							D
R															D
A	■	K	E	E	L	B	A	C	K	■	V	I	P	E	R

(hexagon figure: 1—6, 2, 8—5, 4—9, 1, 5—2)

Answers to The Adventure of the Dancing Men

1. ☞ Letters spell: DECIPHERING. *Go to #5 on map.*

2. ☞ 6 people left several footprints, each with their left and right shoes. *Go to #6 on map.*

3. ☞ The coded message reads: ELSIE PREPARE TO MEET THY GOD. *Go to #12 on map.*

4. ☞ Three pairs of squares were exchanged. *Go to #15 on map.*

5. ☞ 13 different symbols. 13 + 1 = 14. The unique symbols are:

Go to #14 on map.

6. 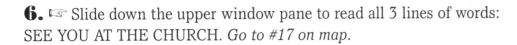 Slide down the upper window pane to read all 3 lines of words: SEE YOU AT THE CHURCH. *Go to #17 on map.*

7. ☞ Every new line uses different letters: PORPOISE - BAT - HEDGEHOG - MINK - VOLE - MUNTJAC - FOX - DEER - STOAT. *Go to #9 on map.*

8. ☞ CHICAGO. 3 + 1 = 4. *Go to #4 on map.*

9. ☞ 3 triplets. 3 × 6 = 18. *Go to #18 on map.*

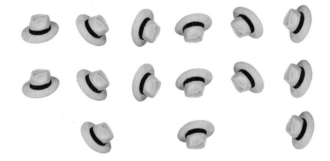

10. ☞ 4 clockwise x 3 counterclockwise. *Go to #20 on map.*

11. ☞ There is no X for WROXHAM. *Go to #10 on map.*

Answers to The Adventure of the Dancing Men

12. ☞ The rings come in 4 sizes and their numbers are 16 - 17 - 18 - 20. The last number should logically be 19 instead of 20. *Go to #21 on map.*

13. ☞ Menu: HAM TIMBALES
GREEN PEAS
CREAMED LEEKS
BAKED SALMON
ROAST CHICKEN
LEMON SHERBET
Go to #19 on map.

14. ☞ Elsie should ensure that he wears a hat: Being a country squire and sometimes angry, he is a blue-eyed person. With a hat, he can be entrusted with her secret. *Go to #3 on map.*

15. ☞ One out of the nine pieces doesn't fit with its neighbors: the southward rectangle. *Go to #11 on map.*

$$9\,5\,6\,7$$
$$+\,1\,0\,8\,5$$
$$\overline{1\,0\,6\,5\,2}$$

16. ☞ The resulting sum is five digits so the addition must mean that the first digit of the sum is 1. The first digit of the second line is the same. The first line, therefore, must begin with 9 to make 10. This also makes the second digit of the third line a 0. The second digit of line two is also a 0. The second digit in line one and the third digit in line three are different, even though a 0 is added to them, meaning that the column to the right must produce a carried 1; these must be two numbers like 2 and 3, or 3 and 4. Testing all possibilities, in addition to the other times these characters appear, only 5 and 6 work. Simply follow addition to determine the other numbers. *Go to #22 on map.*

17. ☞ Here is one of several possible solutions: *Go to #13 on map.*

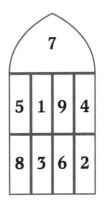

18. ☞ FIRST OF ALL I WANT YOU GENTLEMEN TO UNDERSTAND THAT I HAVE KNOWN THIS LADY SINCE SHE WAS A CHILD. THERE WERE SEVEN OF US IN A GANG IN CHICAGO, AND ELSIE'S FATHER WAS THE BOSS OF THE JOINT. HE WAS A CLEVER MAN, WAS OLD PATRICK. IT WAS HE WHO INVENTED THAT WRITING, WHICH WOULD PASS AS A CHILD'S SCRAWL UNLESS YOU JUST HAPPENED TO HAVE THE KEY TO IT. WELL, ELSIE LEARNED SOME OF OUR WAYS BUT SHE COULDN'T STAND THE BUSINESS AND SHE HAD A BIT OF HONEST MONEY OF HER OWN, SO SHE GAVE US ALL THE SLIP AND GOT AWAY TO LONDON.

Go to #23 on map.

19. ☞ Slaney, the villain, doesn't fit. *Go to #16 on map.*

20. ☞ This triplet has no common symbol with any other. *Go to #2 on map.*

21. ☞ *Go to #8 on map.*

```
          C
    H     U
    A     B
M A R T I N
    G     T
T H U R S T O N
    E
    A
    V
    E
```

22. ☞ MEET ME AT THE WATERING HOLE. *Go to #7 on map.*

23. ☞ SALTPETER (4-letter jumps).

Answers to A Scandal in Bohemia

1. ☞ The main part of the pipe stem, on the far right, is reversed. *Go to #22 on map.*

2. ☞ Godfrey moved each letter forward in the alphabet, alternately by 1 and 2. Moving them back gives "MARRYING IRENE ADLER." Irene Adler totals 10 letters. *Go to #10 on map.*

3. ☞ The steps alternately display two series:
- one with a constant increment of 4: 13, 17, 21 ...
- one with a regularly increasing increment of 3, 4, 5 ... that is: 12, 15, 19, 24 ...
The last step belongs to the increasing increment series and should be 54 + 10 = 64. *Go to #9 on map.*

4. ☞ This series strings the necklace without any common letter when two gemstones are in contact: AMETHYST, ZIRCON, PLASMA, CHERT, DIAMOND, BERYL, TOPAZ, RUBY, SPINEL, QUARTZ, ONYX, JASPER, FLINT, SARD, IOLITE. *Go to #6 on map.*

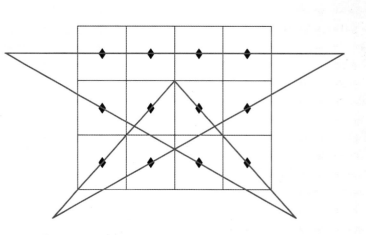

5. ☞ A closed circuit of five lines. *Go to #23 on map.*

6. ☞ In the subset, all of the letters in each pelt's name is different. The sixth one is MARTEN: M is the thirteenth letter. *Go to #13 on map.*

7. ☞ Let's focus on the gear teeth. When the first wheel turns 1 tooth, every other wheel turns 1 tooth, too. When it rotates a full circle, it turns 24 teeth, and so does the last wheel, which means 24 / 12 = 2 full circles. *Go to #17 on map.*

24 teeth

12 teeth

8. ☞ There are 4 complete broughams. *Go to #4 on map.*

9. ☞ The letter reads: SEND DIAMOND TO LADY CLOTILDE. The longest word is Clotilde: 8 letters. *Go to #8 on map.*

10. ☞ KNIGHTS TEMPLAR. *Go to #14 on map.*

11. ☞ CONTEMPT is only used once in the grid and is seventh in the list. *Go to #7 on map.*

12. ☞ The quote reads: A SECRET IS SOMETHING YOU SHARE WITH ONLY ONE PERSON AT A TIME (by Michel Audiard). *Go to #16 on map.*

A		S	E	C	R	E	T		I	S		S	O	M	E	T
H	I	N	G		Y	O	U		S	H	A	R	E		W	I
T	H		O	N	L	Y		O	N	E		P	E	R	S	O
N		A	T		A		T	I	M	E						

13. ☞ There are 10 different areas (did you forget the area around the pictures?).
10 x 2 = 20. *Go to #20 on map.*

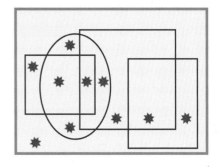

14. ☞ Every number is the product of exactly 2 prime numbers:
21 = 3 x 7
65 = 5 x 13
33 = 3 x 11
...
except 18 = 3 x 3 x 2, a product of 3 prime numbers. *Go to #18 on map.*

15. ☞ On the shelves, there are 6 groups of 6 books, where some volumes are straight, and some are tilted and leaning against the left ones. In every group, there are 4 thick books and 2 thin ones, except in the bottom-right group. *Go to #3 on map.*

16. ☞ The place mentioned is Irene Adler's villa.
Go to #19 on map.

17. ☞ The heart and diamond pips are black instead of red; the spade and club pips are red instead of black. *Go to #21 on map.*

18. ☞ I is contiguous to one R, contiguous to one E, and that E is not contiguous to N. IRENE and ADLER cannot be read on series of contiguous faces.
Go to #5 on map.

19. ☞ The message can bearly be understood, but it includes the word TEMPLE (mentioned by Holmes in the previous puzzle). The entire message reads: I JUST LEFT THE TEMPLE IN A HURRY TO MARRY YOU IMMEDIATELY AT THE CLOSEST CHURCH. *Go to #2 on map.*

20. ☞ Read in this order, the assertions prove that Cheshire Cats don't talk inconsideratly, which prevents them from breaking confidence, hence secrets:

CHESHIRE CATS SMILE NATURALLY.

NO CREATURE EVER SMILES THAT IS NOT COMPASSIONATE.

COMPASSION GENERATES RESPECT.

RESPECT PRECLUDES INCONSIDERATE TALKING.

ONLY LOOSE LIPS BREAK A CONFIDENCE.

ALL SECRETS ARE CONFIDENTIAL.
Go to #12 on map.

21. ☞ Place the seeds in a row and get 10 different alignments of 3:
ABC - ABD - ABE - ACD - ACE - ADE - BCD - BCE - BDE - CDE. *Go to #15 on map.*

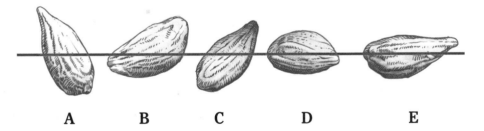

    A   **B**   **C**   **D**   **E**

22. ☞ A, B, and C are gridlocked, each ring blocking the other two, but D, which is above C and under A, can float away freely. *Go to #11 on map.*

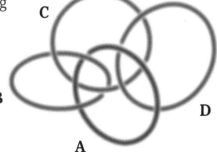

23. ☞ The center piece comes from another paragraph, further in the text.

Answers to The Hound of the Baskervilles

1. ☞ Instead of laying all 6 matches on the table, make a triangle with 3 of them and use the other 3 to complete a four-sided pyramid. *Go to #10 on map.*

2. ☞ HARP, LUTE, FIDDLE, SPINET, GUITAR, LYRE, BANJO, CELLO. FACES does not refer to an instrument. *Go to #12 on map.*

3. ☞ If you superimpose the windows, the candles look like the hands of a watch, and the message reads: "LET'S MEET AT FIVE AFTER TEN." *Go to #21 on map.*

4. ☞ 7 math symbols are needed:
$((3 \times 9) \times (25 \times 4)) + ((7 + 1) / (8 - 6)) = 2704$. *Go to #19 on map.*

5. ☞ : YEW CHERRY HAWTHORN LINDEN JUNIPER POPLAR BIRCH WILLOW. *Go to #2 on map.*

E	C	A	D	E	A	B	I
W	E	**H**	E	I	L	C	L
Y	H	H	I	J	O	**H**	L
R	N	L	N	**P**	I	O	
R	O	N	**P**	P	R	**W**	
Y	R	N	R	R		**W**	
	T		U				
W							

6. ☞ Weeding weeds unwanted letters form INSECTS. *Go to #15 on map.*

7. ☞ Yes, imagination is necessary to be horror stricken: Horror is unbearable, which brings panic, which brings fear, which needs a conscience of danger, which needs a perception of threats, which needs an awareness of consequences, brought by imagination. Therefore, no horror if no imagination. *Go to #22 on map.*

8. ☞ Observe that all numbers of minutes in the right colums are between 1 and 26. Supposing they are the ranks of letters in the alphabet, you get: "KEEP GATE CLOSED." *Go to #20 on map.*

9. ☞ The path. *Go to #6 on map.*

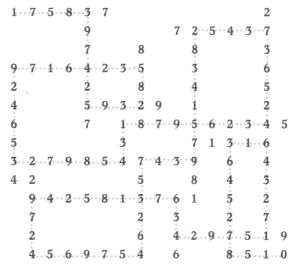

```
1  7  5  8  3  7                              2
         9              7  2  5  4  3  7
         7        8        8              3
9  7  1  6  4  2  3  5     3              6
2              2        8     4           5
4              5  9  3  2  9  1           2
6        7  1  8  7  9  5  6  2  3  4  5
5              3           7  1  3  1  6
3  2  7  9  8  5  4  7  4  3  9     6     4
4  2              5        8     4        3
9  4  2  5  8  1  3  7  6  1     5        2
7                 2     3        2  7
2                 6        4  2  9  7  5  1  9
4  5  6  9  7  5  4        6        8  5  1  0
```

10. ☞ 14 steps. *Go to #14 on map.*

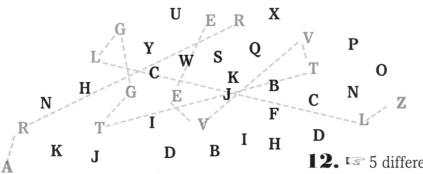

11. ☞ The left T links to 3 Os, each yielding 2 TORs; the middle T to 4 Os, each yielding 2 TORs; and the right to 2 Os, each yielding 2 TORs. We get a sum of 3 x 2 + 4 x 2 + 2 x 2 = 18 TORs. *Go to #18 on map.*

12. ☞ 5 different faces. 5 + 4 = 9. *Go to #9 on map.*

Answers to The Hound of the Baskervilles

13. ☞ FREEDOM replaces REASON: 7 letters. 7 + 10 = 17. *Go to #17 on map.*

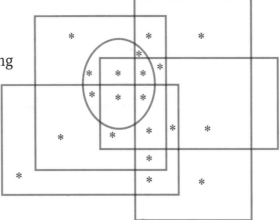

as you value your
life or your
freedom keep away
from the moor

14. ☞ Description reads: "BLAZING EYES AND DRIPPING JAW." *Go to #7 on map.*

```
B L A Z I
N G E Y E
S A N D D
R I P P I
N G J A W
```

15. ☞ One of several possible solutions:
ANT, BEETLE, MOSQUITO, WASP, WEEVIL, BUTTERFLY, LOCUST, MAYFLY, MOTH, CRICKET, APHID, GNAT, SCARAB, TERMITE, (ANT). *Go to #11 on map.*

16. ☞ Cube spells: PHOSPHORUS. *Go to #23 on map.*

17. ☞ 4 knots: each string is knotted twice (and they are interlocked). *Go to #4 on map.*

18. ☞ The keyword is COUNTERCLOCKWISE. *Go to #13 on map.*

19. ☞ There are 21 nonoverlapping zones. *Go to #8 on map.*

20. ☞ Consider the numbers made up of a digit on the left panel and a digit in the same place on the right panel: 14, 21, 28, etc. They are multiples of 7, except 12. 1 + 2 = 3. *Go to #13 on map.*

21. ☞ The message reads: "BURN THIS LETTER AND BE BY TEN AT THE GATE."
Go to #16 on map.

22. ☞ The word is: CURSE.
Go to #5 on map.

23. ☞ The missing scent is: JESSAMINE.

```
A  B  J  V  E  T  I  V  E  J  E  A
G  E  R  G  A  M  O  T  E  H  C
A  M  S  U  V  E  B  E  W  S  I  E
R  Y  S  A  N  D  A  L  W  S  O  D
G  R  A  F  R  O  S  E  N  A  E  A
A  R  M  O  N  X  I  M  C  M  L  R
L  H  I  L  K  A  L  I  A  I  K  O
B  E  N  A  X  L  P  O  R  N  I  S
A  J  E  S  S  A  M  I  N  E  L  E
N  A  L  P  R  E  D  N  E  V  A  L
U  P  X  I  L  U  O  H  C  T  A  P
M  L  K  N  E  X  K  S  I  R  R  O
L  A  V  E  N  D  E  R  K  K  X  A  L
```

Answers to The Red-Headed League

1. ☞ CANDY is not among the shades.
Go to #10 on map.

2. ☞ In each piece, 12 squares remain intact.
Go to #12 on map.

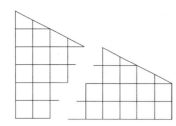 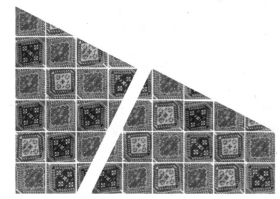

3. ☞ Read A for Ace, B for 2, C for 3, etc.
This yields "HIDE A BAG." *Go to #8 on map.*

4. ☞ The bottom left piece doesn't
fit. The 5 other pieces total 16 squares.
$16 + 3 = 19$. *Go to #19 on map.*

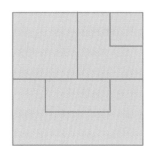 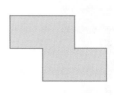

5. ☞ There are 3 different fingerprints. *Go to #20 on map.*

6. ☞ HOUSEBREAKING (13 letters) is only in the top grid. Repeated terms include:
THIEF, SMASHER, FORGER, FRAUD, VILLAIN, OFFENCE, FELON, CROOK,
TRAITOR, RACKETEER, SWINDLER, ARSON, and HUSTLE. *Go to #13 on map.*

7. ☞ ATFNDULPZ
Go to #23 on map.

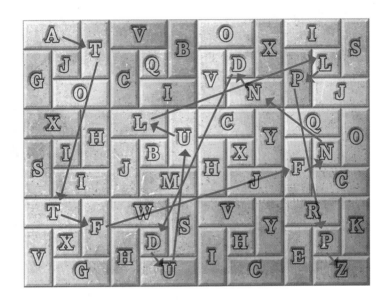

8. ☞ A genius is creative, hence daydreams, hence loves poetry, hence can't hate music. On the contrary, a red-head is witless if adamant, hence hates music if sporting long hair. Hating music, a long-haired adamant red-head cannot be a genius. *Go to #16 on map.*

9. ☞ Let's call the locks A, B, and C. Then give keys A and B to one person, keys B and C to the second person and keys C and A to the third person, a total of 6 keys. Thus, any single person can only open 2 locks, but any two people can open the 3 locks. 6 x 3 = 18. *Go to #18 on map.*

10. ☞ PAWNBROKER (3-letter jumps). *Go to #22 on map.*

11. ☞ One possible solution is: IDIOT, CHUMP, FOOL, CRETIN, DUMMY, CLOT, NINNY, CLOD, PRAT, DUNCE, BOZO, STUPID, GOOF, TWIT, BERK, HALFWIT, MORON. Longest synonym: HALFWIT has 7 letters. *Go to #7 on map.*

12. ☞ The three goods are silver, gold, and a ruby.
Silver is the least expensive and Alex didn't buy it.
Bert, spending more than somebody else, didn't buy silver.
So only Caleb could have bought silver.
Bert, spending more than gold, bought the ruby.
Only Alex could have bought gold.
Since Alex = 4, 4 + 1 = 5. *Go to #5 on map.*

13. ☞
*Go to #11
on map.*

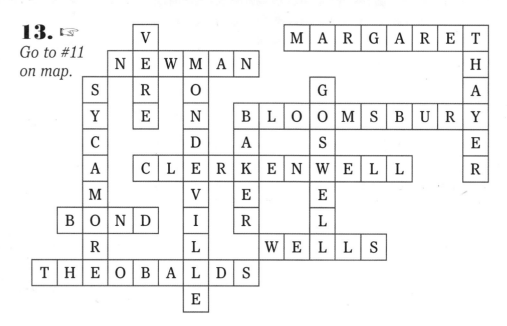

14. ☞ Let's call the first four coins from top left ABCD. The series cycles through them thus: ABCD BCDA CDAB DABC. The fifteenth is the first misplaced coin: C instead of B. *Go to #15 on map.*

15. ☞ 1853, for there is 1 four-pointed star, 8 five-pointed stars, 5 six-pointed stars, and 3 seven-pointed stars. *Go to #3 on map.*

16. ☞ Read the cards horizontally, line after line, starting with the ace of clubs. The pip value increases by increments of 1 for clubs, 2 for diamonds, 3 for spades, and 4 for hearts. Card values "go around the corner," beginning at 1 beyond 10: 9 + 4 = 3.
The value of the hidden card is 10 + 2 (clubs) = 1. Since the following card is a 3, a diamond would have added 2. 1 + 3 = 4. *Go to #4 on map.*

17. ☞ There is no 3, so the 7 is left alone with no complement to 10. 7 x 2 = 14. *Go to #14 on map.*

18. ☞ Put together the discrepant uppercase letters to get "HERE AT TEN." *Go to #21 on map.*

19. ☞ 6 coins, cut up like this: *Go to #6 on map.*

20. ☞ Starting at 4, the minutes increase alternately by 3, and by an increasing number: 5, 6, 7, 8, 9.
4 + 3 = 7; + 5 = 12; + 3 = 15; + 6 = 21; + 3 = 24; + 7 = 31; + 3 = 34; + 8 = 42; + 3 = 45. The new hand would point at 45 + 9 = 54 minutes. 54 / 6 = 9. *Go to #9 on map.*

21. ☞ This time, put together the letters *following* the discrepant uppercase ones to obtain: "BULLION HERE FOUR WEEKS." 4 + 13 = 17. *Go to #17 on map.*

To THE RED-HEADED LEAGUE. - On account of the **B**eq**U**est of the **L**ate Ezekiah Hopkins, o**F** **L**ebanon, Penn., U.S.A. thre **I**s n**O**w a**N**other vacancy open w**H**ich entitl**E**s a membe**R** of th**E** League to a salary o**F** f**O**ur po**U**nds a week fo**R** purely nominal services. All red-headed men who are sound in body and mind, and above the age of t**W**enty-one years, are eligible. Apply in person on Monday, at el**E**v**E**n o'cloc**K**, to Duncan Ro**S**s, at the offices of the League, 7 Pope's Court, Fleet Street.

22. ☞ Each price equals the number of vowels multiplied by the number of consonnants. So the ormolu costs 3 x 3 = 9. *Go to #2 on map.*

23. ☞ Each window "frames" a letter: it shows the preceding and following letters in the alphabet (i.e., GI for H) to yield: "HE DUG A TUNNEL."

Answers to The Adventure of the Naval Treaty

1. ☞ The fumes spell: "GUILTY." *Go to #20 on map.*

2. ☞ In all four quadrants of the backgammon board, except in the top right, the number of checkers are 1, 2, 3, and 4. *Go to #14 on map.*

3. ☞ The precept reads: "THE SUPREME ART OF WAR IS TO SUBDUE THE ENEMY WITHOUT FIGHTING." *Go to #22 on map.*

T	H	E		S	U	P	R	E	M	E		A	R	T		O
F		W	A	R		I	S		T	O			U	B	D	U
E		T	H	E		E	N	E	M	Y		W	I	T	H	O
U	T		F	I	G	H	T	I	N	G						

4. ☞ In this series, none of the following names have a common letter: NAPOLEON, TWIST, DUCHER, SITKA, BOLERO, VANITY, CHUCKLES, ADAM, ERFURT, ALOHA, SPICE, DORTMUND, ALBA, PINKIE, MOZART. *Go to #15 on map.*

5. ☞ Label each segment as A, B, C, and D. Consider first A and B. A can fold over B or underneath it. Likewise, D can fold over C or underneath it, yielding 2 x 2 = 4 possibilities. Then you can either
- fold AB over CD
- fold AB beneath CD
- fold AB between C and D
- fold CD between A and B
  This comes to 4 x 4 = 16 possibilities.
Go to #16 on map.

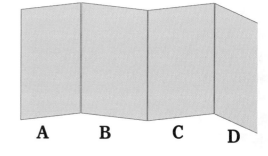

A   **B**   **C**   **D**

6. ☞ Two equal parts are:
Go to #8 on map.

7. ☞ The letters read: "WHITEHALL SIGNS NAVAL TREATY WITH FRANCE AND ITALY." *Go to # 11 on map.*

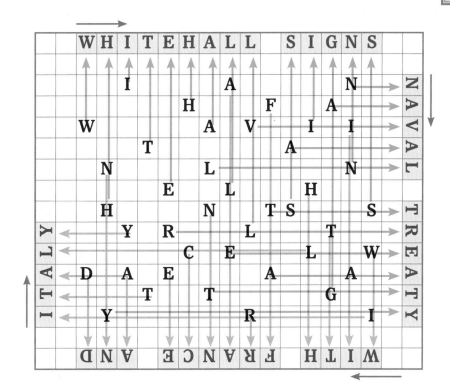

8. ☞ The locket reads: "STOCK MARKET." *Go to #4 on map.*

9. ☞ 3 knots: *Go to # 3 on map.*

10. ☞ *HMS Jumna* cannot be written: there is no U among the floating letters. *Go to # 7 on map.*

11. ☞ Replacing red letters with ones that make sensible words, the hidden message reads: "WAIT FOR A RING." *Go to #21 on map.*

A £10 Reward. - The number of the cab which dropped a fare at or about the door of the Foreign Office in Charles Street, at a quarter to ten in the evening of May 23rd. Apply 221B Baker Street

12. ☞ Every letter is in two different areas, except K, N, O, T, and S, which are only in one. *Go to #9 on map.*

13. ☞ Let's suppose the round trip at an average speed of 12 knots takes 4 days. While traveling the outgoing trip, which is half the distance at 6 knots, the merchant spent 4 days. Having already spent the 4 days on the outgoing trip, the merchant has no time left to manage the return trip. The challenge cannot be met. *Go to #18 on map.*

14. ☞ Stripping away all letters that are not Roman numerals, yields MMLX, meaning 1000 + 1000 + 50 + 10 = 2560. *Go to #7 on map.*

15. ☞ The twelfth possibility: *Go to #5 on map.*

16. ☞ Let's start from the central L and count the LAVANs instead of the NAVALs.
L connects to the above A, that connects to 2 possible VANs.
Above and below give a total of 4 LAVANs.
On the left, A connects to 6 possible VANs.
Left and right A give a total of 12 LAVANs.
NAVAL can be read in 16 different ways. *Go to #2 on map.*

17. ☞ If 7 and 10 switch places, each row, column, and diagonal of the square totals 34. Therefore, cover 16 conceals the missing document. *Go to #23 on map.*

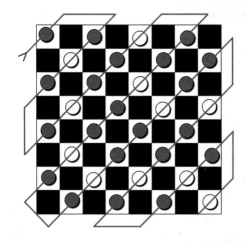

18. ☞ The checkers are placed along the broken diagonal, from top left to bottom right, alternating 2 black checkers with 1 white checker. The last bottom-right checker should be black. *Go to #10 on map.*

19. ☞ MASTER doesn't fit: *Go to #13 on map.*

```
C       B O A T S W A I N     S
H               R             S U
A       R O P E M A K E R       R
P U R S E R         O           G
L     E     Y       U           E
A   C A R P E N T E R     C O O K
I   M       O       E     L     N
N   S A I L M A K E R     E
    N       A             R
    N         C A U L K E R
```

20. ☞ Both squares contain: FLANKER, GENOA, JIB, LATEEN, MIZZEN, and ROYAL. The LUGSAIL is found in the left square only. *Go to #6 on map.*

21. ☞ The time is twelve o'clock. Drawing lines that join the misplaced squares gives the Roman number XII. *Go to #12 on map.*

22. ☞ By extending the lines outside of the sixteen-point square, a closed grouping of six straight lines can be achieved. *Go to #19 on map.*

23. ☞ PERCY'S ROOM (3-letter jumps).

Final Word Puzzle Answer

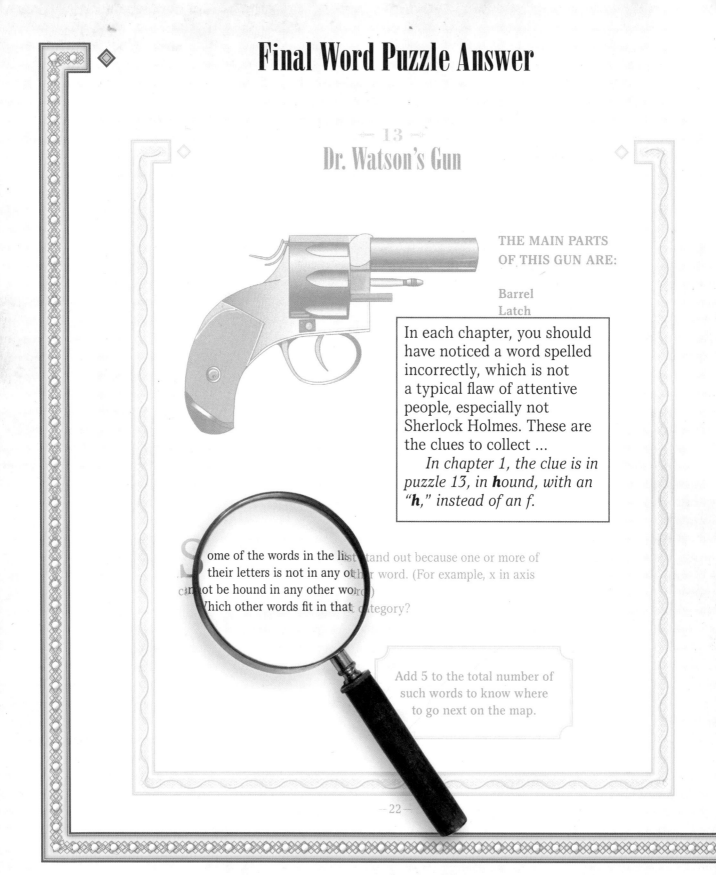

13
Dr. Watson's Gun

THE MAIN PARTS
OF THIS GUN ARE:

Barrel
Latch

In each chapter, you should
have noticed a word spelled
incorrectly, which is not
a typical flaw of attentive
people, especially not
Sherlock Holmes. These are
the clues to collect ...

*In chapter 1, the clue is in
puzzle 13, in **h**ound, with an
"**h**," instead of an f.*

ome of the words in the list stand out because one or more of
their letters is not in any other word. (For example, x in axis
cannot be hound in any other word.)
Which other words fit in that category?

Add 5 to the total number of
such words to know where
to go next on the map.

— 22 —

mge!" shouts Holm...
these dancing figures
ndial?
ge of the dansing men

*In chapter 2, the clue is in puzzle 22, in dan**s**ing, with an **s** instead of a c.*

*nore distant pla**g**es are*
horizontal and vertica...
...n, with only five
..."

*In chapter 3, the clue is in puzzle 5, in pla**g**es, with a **g** instead of a c.*

...became so famous w...
...rville that its descripti...
...e three squares of glass...
...it says, Wotson?"

*In chapter 4, the clue is in puzzle 14, in W**o**tson, with an **o** instead of an a.*

...on, our client has h...
...rhood's meetings.
*...bols displa**s**ed on the a...*
...on?"

*In chapter 5, the clue is in puzzle 15, in displa**s**ed, with an **s** instead of a c.*

A nother p...
which ca...
folting a four-part ma...
"How many ways

*In chapter 6, the clue is in puzzle 5, in fol**t**ed, with a **t** instead of a d.*

You found the letters **HSGOST** as hidden mistakes in the six chapters. In the right order, they form the word: **GHOSTS**.

These entities were an important reference for Sir Arthur Conan Doyle. All his life he was interested in two conflicting domains of creation and research: logic and the supernatural. On one hand, he created Sherlock Holmes, the most logical person ever imagined; on the other hand, he wrote authentic horror stories that did not end with logical explanations such as *The Hound of the Baskervilles,* where phosphorus causes the dog's fiery appearance. On the contrary, his horror stories often suppose that unexplained phenomena do take place.

Sir Arthur often took part in seances where spirits, fairies, and ghosts commonly appeared before his eyes. He never accepted that he had been tricked by fake mediums, yet he always insisted on applying the strictest scientific methods to analyze their supernatural experiments. This means he never forgot his early medical education and practice, which taught him both to face the unexpected aspects of reality and to use scientific tools to deal with them.

Finally, weren't Doctor Watson and Sherlock Holmes, in fact, two faces of one person rather than companions: Sir Arthur Conan Doyle—both author and doctor, creator of mysteries as well as dedicated to solving them?

Puzzle Map Answers

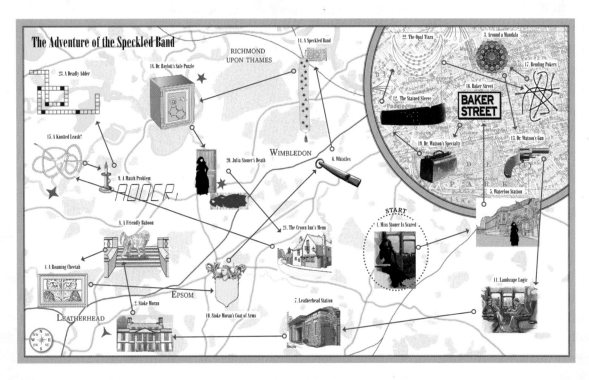

The Adventure of the Speckled Band

- 23. A Deadly Adder
- 18. Dr. Roylott's Safe Puzzle
- 14. A Speckled Band
- 22. The Opal Tiara
- 3. Around a Mandala
- 17. Bending Pokers
- 15. A Knotted Leash?
- 12. The Stained Sleeve
- 16. Baker Street
- 13. Dr. Watson's Gun
- 9. A Match Problem
- 20. Julia Stoner's Death
- 19. Dr. Watson's Specialty
- 6. Whistles
- 5. Waterloo Station
- 8. A Friendly Baboon
- 21. The Crown Inn's Menu
- 1. Miss Stoner Is Scared
- 4. A Roaming Cheetah
- 11. Landscape Logic
- 2. Stoke Moran
- 10. Stoke Moran's Coat of Arms
- 7. Leatherhead Station

RICHMOND UPON THAMES
WIMBLEDON
EPSOM
LEATHERHEAD
START

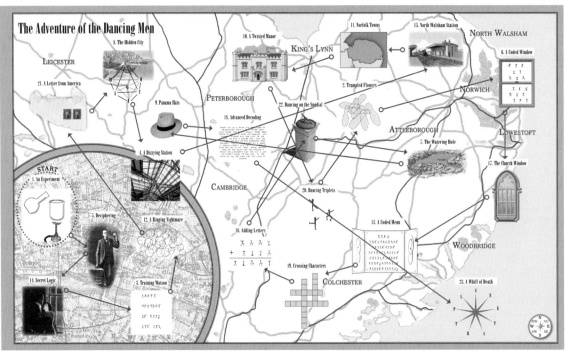

The Adventure of the Dancing Men

- 8. The Hidden City
- 10. A Twisted Manor
- 11. Norfolk Towns
- 15. North Walsham Station
- 6. A Coded Window
- 21. A Letter from America
- 9. Panama Hats
- 2. Trampled Flowers
- 18. Advanced Decoding
- 22. Dancing on the Sundial
- 7. The Watering Hole
- 4. A Dizzying Station
- 20. Dancing Triplets
- 17. The Church Window
- 1. An Experiment
- 5. Deciphering
- 12. A Ringing Nightmare
- 16. Adding Letters
- 13. A Coded Menu
- 19. Crossing Characters
- 14. Secret Logic
- 3. Training Watson
- 23. A Whiff of Death

LEICESTER
KING'S LYNN
NORTH WALSHAM
PETERBOROUGH
NORWICH
ATTLEBOROUGH
LOWESTOFT
CAMBRIDGE
WOODBRIDGE
COLCHESTER
START

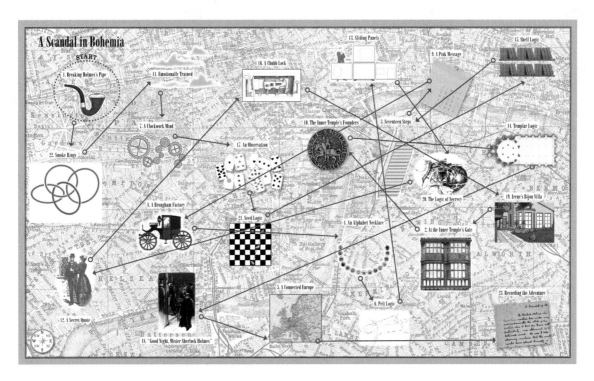

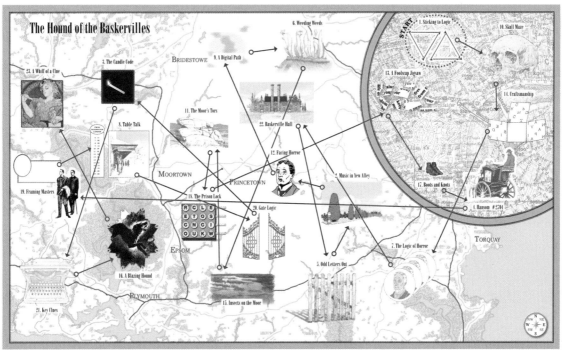

Puzzle Map Answers

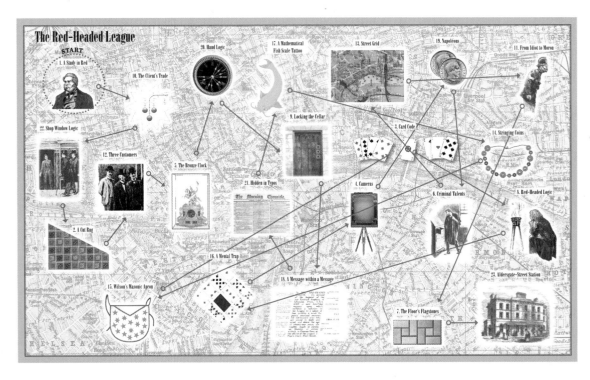

The Red-Headed League

START
1. A Study in Red
10. The Client's Trade
20. Hand Logic
17. A Mathematical Fish Scale Tattoo
13. Street Grid
19. Napoleons
11. From Idiot to Moron
22. Shop Window Logic
9. Locking the Cellar
3. Card Code
14. Stringing Coins
12. Three Customers
5. The Bronze Clock
21. Hidden in Typos
4. Cameras
6. Criminal Talents
8. Red-Headed Logic
2. A Cut Rug
16. A Mental Trap
18. A Message within a Message
23. Aldersgate-Street Station
15. Wilson's Masonic Apron
7. The Floor's Flagstones

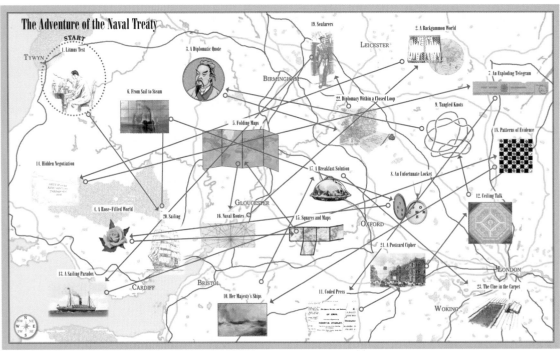

The Adventure of the Naval Treaty

START
1. Litmus Test
TYWYN
3. A Diplomatic Quote
19. Seafarers
LEICESTER
2. A Backgammon World
7. An Exploding Telegram
6. From Sail to Steam
BIRMINGHAM
22. Diplomacy Within a Closed Loop
9. Tangled Knots
5. Folding Maps
18. Patterns of Evidence
14. Hidden Negotiation
17. A Breakfast Solution
8. An Unfortunate Locket
12. Ceiling Talk
4. A Rose-Filled World
20. Sailing
16. Naval Routes
15. Squares and Maps
GLOUCESTER
OXFORD
21. A Postcard Cipher
13. A Sailing Paradox
BRISTOL
CARDIFF
11. Coded Press
10. Her Majesty's Ships
LONDON
23. The Clue in the Carpet
WOKING

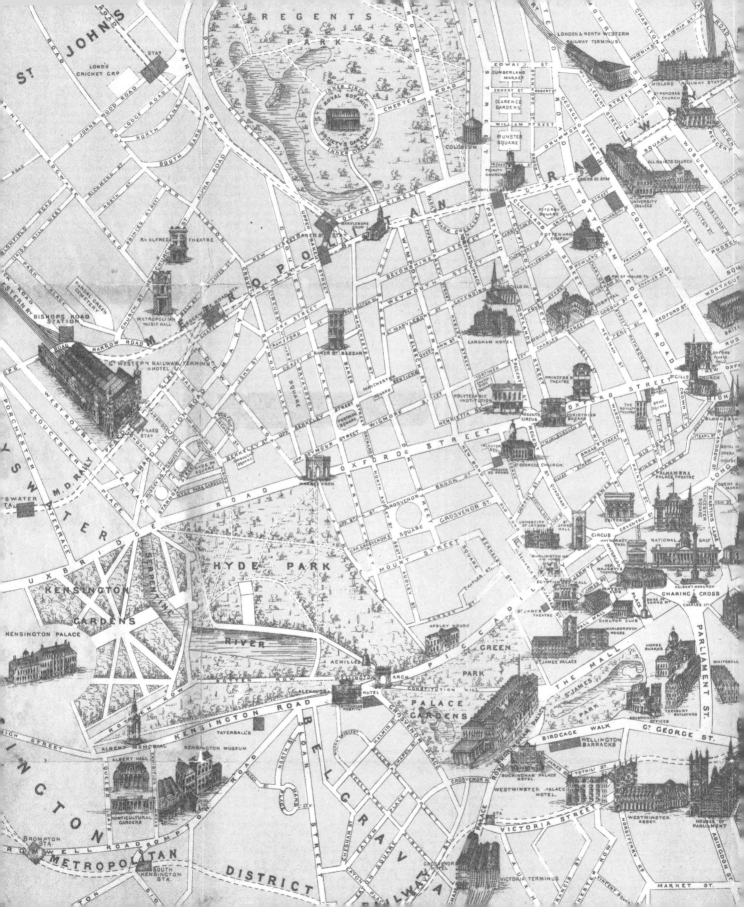